# ARKANSAS NURSING LAW:
## PRACTICE ACT,
## RULES & REGULATIONS,
## AND BOARD POSITION STATEMENTS

### 2010 – 2011 Edition

Law Offices of Lisa Douglas, Inc.
2300 Main Street
North Little Rock, AR 72114
(501) 798-0004
www.LisaGDouglas.com
LisaGDouglas@aol.com

# FOREWARD

Special thanks to John Wesley Hall, criminal defense attorney, in Best Lawyers in America–Criminal Defense, without whose help, this book would not be complete. His research and editorial suggestions have proven invaluable, and I thank him for spending untold hours in production of this final product. I could not have come this far without him. He is of counsel to my law firm—an accomplished trial and appellate lawyer, legal scholar, author of legal treatises through Lexis Law Publishing, West Publishing Company, and published by himself. He has tried over 300 jury trials, a war crimes trial, written over 250 appeals briefs, and argued twice in the United States Supreme Court. He is the guy who handles the criminal cases that come to this office.

# TABLE OF CONTENTS

## PART I
## ARKANSAS NURSE PRACTICE ACT

Professions, Occupations and Businesses, Title 17

Chapter 87. Nurses

Subchapter 1. General Provisions

Subchapter 2. Arkansas State Board of Nursing

Subchapter 3. Licensing

**PART II**
**ARKANSAS STATE BOARD OF**
**NURSING RULES AND REGULATIONS**

CHAPTER ONE – GENERAL PROVISIONS

CHAPTER TWO – LICENSURE: RN, LPN, AND LPTN

CHAPTER THREE – REGISTERED NURSE PRACTITIONER

# CHAPTER FOUR – ADVANCED PRACTICE NURSING

# CHAPTER FIVE – DELEGATION

# CHAPTER SIX – MINIMUM REQUIREMENTS FOR NURSING EDUCATION PROGRAMS

# CHAPTER SEVEN – RULES OF PROCEDURE

# CHAPTER EIGHT – MEDICATION ASSISTANT-CERTIFIED

# PART III
## POSITION STATEMENTS OF THE
## ARKANSAS STATE BOARD OF NURSING

# PART I

# ARKANSAS NURSE PRACTICE ACT
### Arkansas Code, Title 17, Chapter 87

## Subchapter 1 – General Provisions

### § 17-87-101.  License Required-Purpose

(a)  In order to safeguard life and health, any person practicing or offering to practice nursing for compensation shall be required to submit evidence that he or she is qualified to so practice and shall be licensed as provided in this chapter:

(1)  Professional nursing;

(2)  Advanced practice nursing;

(3)  Registered practitioner nursing;

(4)  Practical nursing; or

(5)  Psychiatric technician nursing.

(b)  It shall be unlawful for any person not licensed by the board:

(1)  To practice or offer to practice professional nursing, advanced practice nursing, registered practitioner nursing, practical nursing, or psychiatric technician nursing; or

(2)  To use any sign, card, or device to indicate that the person is a professional registered nurse, an advanced practice nurse, a registered nurse practitioner, a licensed practical nurse, or a licensed psychiatric technician nurse.

**History:**

Acts 1971, No. 432, § 1; 1979, No. 613, § 1; 1980 (1st Ex. Sess.), No. 14, § 1; A.S.A. 1947, § 72-745; 1995, No. 409, § 1.

### § 17-87-102.  Definitions

As used in this chapter:

**(1)** "Board" means the Arkansas State Board of Nursing;

**(2)** "Collaborative practice agreement" means a written plan that identifies a physician who agrees to collaborate with an advanced practice nurse in the joint management of the health care of the advanced practice nurse's patients, and outlines procedures for consultation with or referral to the collaborating physician or other health care professionals as indicated by a patient's health care needs;

**(3)** "Consulting physician" means a physician licensed under the Arkansas Medical Practices Act, §§ 17-95-201–17-95-207, 17-95-301–17-95-305, and 17-95-401–17-95-411, with obstetrical privileges in a hospital, who has agreed to practice in consultation with a certified nurse midwife; and

**(4) (A)** "Practice of advanced practice nursing" means the delivery of health care services for compensation by professional nurses who have gained additional knowledge and skills through successful completion of an organized program of nursing education that certifies nurses for advanced practice roles as advanced nurse practitioners, certified nurse anesthetists, certified nurse midwives, and clinical nurse specialists.

**(B) (I)** "Practice of advanced nurse practitioner nursing" means the performance for compensation of nursing skills by a registered nurse who, as demonstrated by national certification, has advanced knowledge and practice skills in the delivery of nursing services.

**(ii)** "Practice of certified registered nurse anesthesia" means the performance for compensation of advanced nursing skills relevant to the administration of anesthetics under the supervision of, but not necessarily in the presence of, a licensed physician, licensed dentist, or other person lawfully entitled to order anesthesia. A certified registered nurse anesthetist may order nurses, within their scope of practice, to administer drugs preoperatively and postoperatively in connection with an anesthetic or other operative or invasive procedure, or both, that will be or has been provided.

**(iii)** "Practice of clinical nurse specialist nursing" means the performance for compensation of nursing skills by a registered nurse who, through study and supervised practice at the graduate level and as evidenced by national certification, has advanced knowledge and practice skills in a specialized area of nursing practice;

**(iv)** "Practice of nurse midwifery" means the performance for compensation of nursing skills relevant to the management of women's health care, focusing on pregnancy, childbirth, the postpartum period, care of the newborn, family planning, and gynecological needs of women, within a health care system that provides for consultation, collaborative management, or referral as indicated by the health status of the client.

**(5)** "Practice of practical nursing" means the performance for compensation of acts involving the care of the ill, injured, or infirm or the delegation of certain nursing practices

4

to other personnel as set forth in regulations established by the board under the direction of a registered professional nurse, an advanced practice nurse, a licensed physician, or a licensed dentist, which acts do not require the substantial specialized skill, judgment, and knowledge required in professional nursing;

(6) "Practice of professional nursing" means the performance for compensation of any acts involving:

(A) The observation, care, and counsel of the ill, injured, or infirm;

(B) The maintenance of health or prevention of illness of others;

(C) The supervision and teaching of other personnel;

(D) The delegation of certain nursing practices to other personnel as set forth in regulations established by the board; or

(E) The administration of medications and treatments as prescribed by practitioners authorized to prescribe and treat in accordance with state law where such acts require substantial specialized judgment and skill based on knowledge and application of the principles of biological, physical, and social sciences;

(7) "Practice of psychiatric technician nursing" means the performance for compensation of acts involving the care of the physically and mentally ill, retarded, injured, or infirm or the delegation of certain nursing practices to other personnel as set forth in regulations established by the board, and the carrying out of medical orders under the direction of a registered professional nurse, an advanced practice nurse, a licensed physician, or a licensed dentist, where such activities do not require the substantial specialized skill, judgment, and knowledge required in professional nursing; and

(8) (A) "Practice of registered nurse practitioner nursing" means the delivery of health care services for compensation in collaboration with and under the direction of a licensed physician or under the direction of protocols developed with a licensed physician.

(B) Registered nurse practitioners shall be authorized to engage in activities as recognized by the nursing profession and as authorized by the board.

(C) Nothing in this subdivision (8) is to be deemed to limit a registered nurse practitioner from engaging in those activities which normally constitute the practice of nursing, or those which may be performed by persons without the necessity of the license to practice medicine.

**History:**

Acts 1971, No. 432, § 2; 1979, No. 404, §§ 1, 7; 1979, No. 613, § 2; A.S.A. 1947, § 72-746; Acts 1995, No. 409, § 2; 1997, No. 1065, § 1; 1999, No. 1208, § 1.

## § 17-87-103. Exceptions

This chapter does not prohibit:

**(1)** The furnishing of nursing assistance in an emergency;

**(2)** The practice of nursing that is incidental to their program of study by students enrolled in nursing education programs approved by the board;

**(3)** The practice of any legally qualified nurse of another state who is employed by the United States Government or any bureau, division, or agency while in the discharge of his or her official duties in installations where jurisdiction has been ceded by the State of Arkansas;

**(4)** The practice of any legally qualified and licensed nurse of another state, territory, or foreign country whose responsibilities include transporting patients into, out of, or through this state while actively engaged in patient transport that does not exceed forty-eight (48) hours in this state;

**(5)** Nursing or care of the sick when done in connection with the practice of the religious tenets of any church by its adherents;

**(6)** The care of the sick when done in accordance with the practice of religious principles or tenets of any well-recognized church or denomination that relies upon prayer or spiritual means of healing;

**(7)** The administration of anesthetics under the supervision of, but not necessarily in the presence of, a licensed physician, dentist, or other person lawfully entitled to order anesthesia by a graduate nurse anesthetist awaiting certification results while holding a temporary permit;

**(8)** The administration of anesthetics under the supervision of, but not necessarily in the presence of, a licensed physician, dentist, or other person lawfully entitled to order anesthesia by a registered nurse who is enrolled as a bona fide student pursuing a course in a nurse anesthesia school that is approved by a nationally recognized accrediting body and whose graduates are acceptable for certification by a nationally recognized certifying body, provided the giving or administering of the anesthetics is confined to the educational requirements of the course and under the direct supervision of a qualified instructor;

**(9)** Hospital-employed professional paramedics from administering medication for diagnostic procedures under the direction of a physician;

6

**(10)** The prescription and administration of drugs, medicines, or therapeutic devices in the presence of and under the supervision of an advanced practice nurse holding a certificate of prescriptive authority, a licensed physician, or licensed dentist by a registered nurse who is enrolled as a student in an advanced pharmacology course, provided the prescription or administration of drugs or medicines, or both, is confined to the educational requirements of the course and under the direct supervision of a qualified instructor; or

**(11) (A)** Health maintenance activities by a designated care aide for a:

**(i)** Competent adult at the direction of the adult; or

**(ii)** Minor child or incompetent adult at the direction of a caretaker.

**(B)** As used in this section:

**(i)** "Caretaker" means a person who is:

**(*a*)** Directly and personally involved in providing care for a minor child or incompetent adult; and

**(*b*)** The parent, foster parent, family member, friend, or legal guardian of the minor child or incompetent adult receiving care under subdivision (11)(B)(i)(*a* ) of this section;

**(ii)** "Competent adult" means an individual who:

**(*a*)** Is eighteen (18) years of age or older; and

**(*b*)** Has the capability and capacity to make an informed decision; and

**(iii)** "Health maintenance activities" means activities that:

**(*a*)** Enable a minor child or adult to live in his or her home; and

**(*b*)** Are beyond activities of daily living that:

**(*1*)** The minor child or adult is unable to perform for himself or herself; and

**(*2*)** The attending physician, advanced practice nurse, or registered nurse determines can be safely performed in the minor child's or adult's home by a designated care aide under the direction of a competent adult or caretaker.

**(C)** As used in this section, "home" does not include:

**(i)** A nursing home;

**(ii)** An assisted living facility;

**(iii)** A residential care facility;

**(iv)** An intermediate care facility; or

**(v)** A hospice care facility.

**(D)** The Arkansas State Board of Nursing with the input of the Home Health Care Service Agency Advisory Council, the Arkansas Health Care Association, and the Arkansas Residential Assisted Living Association shall promulgate rules specifying which health maintenance activities are not exempted under this subdivision (11) and the minimal qualifications required of the designated care aide.

**History:**

Acts 1971, No. 432, §§ 1, 2, 17; 1979, No. 404, §§ 1, 7; 1979, No. 613, §§ 1, 2; 1980 (1st Ex. Sess.), No. 14, §§ 1, 3; 1985, No. 189, § 2; A.S.A. 1947, §§ 72-745, 72-746, 72-761; Acts 1995, No. 409, § 3; 1997, No. 1065, § 2; 2005, No. 1440, § 1.

## § 17-87-104. Penalty

**(a)** **(1)** It shall be a misdemeanor for any person to:

**(A)** Sell or fraudulently obtain or furnish any nursing diploma, license, renewal, or record, or aid or abet therein;

**(B)** Practice nursing as defined by this chapter under cover of any diploma, license, or record illegally or fraudulently obtained or signed or issued unlawfully or under fraudulent representation;

**(C)** Practice professional nursing, advanced practice nursing, registered nurse practitioner nursing, practical nursing, or psychiatric technician nursing as defined by this chapter unless licensed by the Arkansas State Board of Nursing to do so;

**(D)** Use in connection with his or her name any of the following titles, names, or initials, if the user is not properly licensed under this chapter:

**(i)** Nurse;

**(ii)** Registered nurse or R.N.;

**(iii)** Advanced practice nurse or A.P.N., or any of the following:

    (*a*) Advanced registered nurse practitioner, A.R.N.P., or A.N.P.;

    (*b*) Nurse anesthetist, certified nurse anesthetist, certified registered nurse anesthetist, or C.R.N.A.;

    (*c*) Nurse midwife, certified nurse midwife, licensed nurse midwife, C.N.M., or L.N.M.; or

    (*d*) Clinical nurse specialist or C.N.S.;

**(iv)** Registered nurse practitioner, N.P., or R.N.P.;

**(v)** Licensed practical nurse, practical nurse, or L.P.N.;

**(vi)** Licensed psychiatric technician nurse, psychiatric technician nurse, L.P.T.N., or P.T.N.; or

**(vii)** Any other name, title, or initials that would cause a reasonable person to believe the user is licensed under this chapter;

**(E)** Practice professional nursing, advanced practice nursing, registered nurse practitioner nursing, practical nursing, or psychiatric technician nursing during the time his or her license shall be suspended;

**(F)** Conduct a nursing education program for the preparation of professional nurses, advanced practice nurses, nurse practitioners, practical nurses, or psychiatric technician nurses unless the program has been approved by the board;

**(G)** Prescribe any drug or medicine as authorized by this chapter unless certified by the board as having prescriptive authority, except that a certified registered nurse anesthetist shall not be required to have prescriptive authority to provide anesthesia care, including the administration of drugs or medicines necessary for the care; or

**(H)** Otherwise violate any provisions of this chapter.

**(2)** Such misdemeanor shall be punishable by a fine of not less than twenty-five dollars ($25.00) nor more than five hundred dollars ($500). Each subsequent offense shall be punishable by fine or by imprisonment of not more than thirty (30) days, or by both fine and imprisonment.

**(b) (1)** After providing notice and a hearing, the board may levy civil penalties in an amount not to exceed one thousand dollars ($1000) for each violation against those individuals or entities found to be in violation of this chapter or regulations promulgated thereunder.

**(2)** Each day of violation shall be a separate offense.

**(3)** These penalties shall be in addition to other penalties which may be imposed by the board pursuant to this chapter.

**(4)** Unless the penalty assessed under this subsection is paid within fifteen (15) calendar days following the date for an appeal from the order, the board shall have the power to file suit in the Circuit Court of Pulaski County to obtain a judgment for the amount of penalty not paid.

**History:**

Acts 1971, No. 432, § 18; Acts 1980 (1st Ex. Sess.), No. 14, § 4; A.S.A. 1947, § 72-762; Acts 1995, No. 409, § 4.

## § 17-87-105. Injunction

**(a)** The Circuit Court of Pulaski County is vested with jurisdiction and power to enjoin the unlawful practice of nursing in any county of the State of Arkansas in a proceeding by the board or by any member thereof or by any citizen in this state.

**(b)** The issuance of any injunction shall not relieve a person from criminal prosecution for violation of the provisions of this chapter. The remedy of injunction is to be in addition to liability for criminal prosecution.

**History:**

Acts 1971, No. 432, § 19; A.S.A. 1947, § 72-763.

## § 17-87-106. Construction of Chapter

Nothing in this chapter relating to the practice of advanced practice nursing shall be construed to limit or alter the scope of practice of any registered nurse practitioner or any other licensed nurse.

**History:**

Acts 1995, No. 409, § 21.

## Subchapter 2 – Arkansas State Board of Nursing

### § 17-87-201.  Creation – Members

**(a)** There is created the Arkansas State Board of Nursing, to be composed of thirteen (13) members to be appointed by the Governor for terms of four (4) years, subject to confirmation by the Senate.

**(b) (1)** Six (6) members shall be registered nurses whose highest level of educational preparation shall be as follows:

**(A)** Two (2) diploma-school graduates;

**(B)** Two (2) associate degree graduates; and

**(C)** Two (2) baccalaureate degree or postbaccalaureate degree graduates.

**(2)** Each registered nurse member of the board shall have the following qualifications:

**(A)** Be an Arkansas resident;

**(B)** Have at least five (5) years of successful experience as a registered nurse in nursing practice, administration, or teaching;

**(C)** Be licensed in Arkansas as a registered nurse; and

**(D)** Have been employed as a registered nurse for at least three (3) years immediately preceding appointment, two (2) of which shall have been in Arkansas.

**(c) (1)** One (1) member shall be a licensed advanced practice nurse.

**(2)** The licensed advanced practice nurse board member shall have the following qualifications:

**(A)** Be an Arkansas resident;

**(B)** Have at least five (5) years of experience as an advanced practice nurse;

**(C)** Be licensed in Arkansas as an advanced practice nurse;

**(D)** Have been actively engaged in nursing for at least three (3) years immediately preceding appointment, two (2) of which shall have been in Arkansas; and

**(E)** Have a certificate granting prescriptive authority.

**(d) (1)** Four (4) members shall be licensed practical nurses or licensed psychiatric technician nurses.

**(2)** Each licensed practical nurse board member or licensed psychiatric technician nurse board member shall have the following qualifications:

**(A)** Be an Arkansas resident;

**(B)** Have at least five (5) years of successful experience as a practical nurse or psychiatric technician nurse or as a teacher in an educational program to prepare practitioners of nursing;

**(C)** Be licensed in Arkansas as a licensed practical nurse or licensed psychiatric technician nurse; and

**(D)** Have been employed as a licensed practical nurse or as a licensed psychiatric technician nurse for at least three (3) years immediately preceding appointment, two (2) of which shall have been in Arkansas.

**(e)** One (1) member shall be a lay person representing consumers of health care services.

**(f)** One (1) member of the board shall not be actively engaged in or retired from the profession of nursing, shall be sixty (60) years of age or older, and shall be the representative of the elderly. This member shall be appointed from the state at large, subject to confirmation by the Senate, and shall be a full voting member but shall not participate in the grading of examinations.

**(g)** The consumer representative and the representative of the elderly positions may not be filled by the same person.

**(h)** No member shall be appointed to more than two (2) consecutive terms.

**(i)** Board members may receive expense reimbursement and stipends in accordance with § 25-16-901 et seq.

**(j)** The terms of all registered nurse members and advanced practice nurse members shall be four (4) years.

**History:**

Acts 1971, No. 432, §§ 3, 4; 1977, No. 113, §§ 1-3; 1979, No. 404, §§ 2, 3; 1981, No. 717, § 2; 1983, No. 131, §§ 1-3, 5; 1983, No. 135, §§ 1-3, 5; 1985, No. 189, § 1; A.S.A. 1947, §§ 6-617 — 6-619, 6-623 — 6-626, 72-747, 72-748; Acts 1995, No. 409, § 5; 1997, No. 250, § 159; 1999, No. 941, § 1; 2001, No. 149, §§ 1, 2; 2007, No. 205, § 1.

## § 17-87-202. Organization and Proceedings

**(a) (1)** It shall be the duty of the Arkansas State Board of Nursing to meet regularly at least one (1) time every six (6) months for the purpose of conducting its business.

**(2)** Special meetings of the board may be called at any time at the pleasure of the President of the Arkansas State Board of Nursing or by the Secretary of the Arkansas State Board of Nursing on the request of any three (3) members of the board.

**(3)** A majority of the members shall constitute a quorum at any meeting of the board.

**(4)** The board shall determine by its own rules the time and manner of giving notice of meetings to its members.

**(5)** The giving of an examination for licensure shall not be considered as a meeting of the board.

**(b)** The secretary shall keep a record of the minutes of the meetings of the board, together with a record of the action of the board thereon. The records shall at all reasonable times be open for public inspection.

**(c)** The board shall maintain an office for the administration of its business. The board shall annually elect a president, vice president, secretary, and treasurer from among its members. The president of the board shall be a registered nurse.

**(d)** The executive director of the board shall be a registered nurse and meet the qualifications required by the board.

**History:**

Acts 1971, No. 432, §§ 4, 8, 9; 1979, No. 404, §§ 3, 5, 6; A.S.A. 1947, §§ 72-748, 72-752, 72-753; Acts 2003, No. 41, § 1.

## § 17-87-203. Powers and duties

The Arkansas State Board of Nursing shall have the following powers and responsibilities:

(1) (A) Promulgate whatever regulations it deems necessary for the implementation of this chapter.

(B) No regulation promulgated hereafter by the board shall be effective until reviewed by the Legislative Council and the House Interim Committee on Public Health, Welfare, and Labor and the Senate Interim Committee on Public Health, Welfare, and Labor or appropriate subcommittees thereof;

(2) Cause the prosecution of persons violating this chapter;

(3) Keep a record of all its proceedings;

(4) Make an annual report to the Governor;

(5) Employ personnel necessary for carrying out its functions;

(6) Study, review, develop, and recommend role levels of technical classes of nursing service and practice to state and federal health agencies and to public and private administrative bodies;

(7) Fix the time for holding its regular meetings;

(8) Prescribe minimum standards and approve curricula for educational programs preparing persons for licensure as registered nurses, advanced practice nurses, registered nurse practitioner nurses, licensed practical nurses, and licensed psychiatric technician nurses;

(9) Prescribe minimum standards and approve curricula for educational programs preparing persons for certification as medication assistive persons;

(10) Provide for surveys of such programs at such times as it deems necessary or at the request of the schools;

(11) Approve programs that meet the requirements of this chapter;

(12) Deny or withdraw approval from educational programs for failure to meet prescribed standards;

**(13)** Examine, certify, and renew the certification of qualified applicants for medication assistive persons;

**(14)** Examine, license, and renew the licenses of qualified applicants for professional nursing, practical nursing, and psychiatric technician nursing;

**(15)** License and renew the licenses of qualified applicants for registered nurse practitioner nursing and advanced practice nursing;

**(16)** Grant certificates of prescriptive authority to qualified advanced practice nurses;

**(17)** Convene an advisory committee as provided for in this chapter to assist with oversight of prescriptive authority;

**(18)** Convene an advisory committee as provided for in this chapter to assist with oversight of medication assistive persons;

**(19)** Establish the maximum number of medication assistive persons who may be supervised by a nurse; and

**(20)** Conduct disciplinary proceedings as provided for in this chapter.

**History:**

Acts 1971, No. 432, § 4; 1979, No. 404, § 3; A.S.A. 1947, § 72-748; Acts 1995, No. 409, § 6; 1997, No. 179, § 13; 2005, No. 1423, § 2.

## § 17-87-204.  Deposit of Funds

All funds received by the Arkansas State Board of Nursing shall be deposited in the State Treasury to the credit of the board.

**History:**

Acts 1971, No. 432, § 14; 1979, No. 404, § 4; A.S.A. 1947, § 72-758.

## § 17-87-205. Prescriptive Authority Advisory Committee

**(a) (1)** The Prescriptive Authority Advisory Committee is created as an advisory committee to the Arkansas State Board of Nursing.

**(2)** The committee shall assist the board in implementing the provisions of this chapter regarding prescriptive authority.

**(b)** The board shall appoint five (5) members, to be approved by the Governor, who have the following qualifications:

**(1)** Three (3) members shall be advanced practice nurses holding certificates of prescriptive authority;

**(2)** One (1) member shall be a licensed physician who has been involved in a collaborative practice with a registered nurse practitioner for at least five (5) years; and

**(3)** One (1) member shall be a licensed pharmacist who has been in practice for at least five (5) years.

**(c)** Members shall serve three-year terms.

**(d)** The board may remove any committee member, after notice and hearing, for incapacity, incompetence, neglect of duty, or malfeasance in office.

**(e)** The members shall serve without compensation, but may receive expense reimbursement in accordance with § 25-16-901 et seq.

**History:**

Acts 1995, No. 409, § 7; 1997, No. 250, § 160.

## § 17-87-206. Subpoenas and Subpoena Duces Tecum

**(a)** The Arkansas State Board of Nursing shall have the power to issue subpoenas and subpoenas duces tecum in connection with both its investigations and hearings.

**(b)** A subpoena duces tecum may require any book, writing, document, or other paper or thing which is germane to an investigation or hearing conducted by the board to be transmitted to the board.

**(c) (1)** Service of a subpoena shall be as provided by law for the service of subpoenas in civil cases in the circuit courts of this state, and the fees and mileage of officers serving the subpoenas and of witnesses appearing in answer to the subpoenas shall be the same as provided by law for proceedings in civil cases in the circuit courts of this state.

**(2) (A)** The board shall issue a subpoena or subpoena duces tecum upon the request of any party to a hearing before the board.

**(B)** The fees and mileage of the officers serving the subpoena and of the witness shall be paid by the party at whose request a witness is subpoenaed.

**(d) (1)** In the event a person shall have been served with a subpoena or subpoena duces tecum as provided in this section and fails to comply therewith, the board may apply to the circuit court of the county in which the board is conducting its investigation or hearing for an order causing the arrest of the person and directing that the person be brought before the court.

**(2)** The court shall have the power to punish the disobedient person for contempt as provided by law in the trial of civil cases in the circuit courts of this state.

**History:**

Acts 1997, No. 894, § 1.

## § 17-87-207. Continuing Education

**(a) (1)** The Arkansas State Board of Nursing shall adopt rules setting minimum standards for continuing education to ensure that all licensed nurses remain informed about those technical and professional subjects which the board deems appropriate to nursing practice.

**(2)** The board shall not require more than twenty (20) hours of continuing education per year.

**(b)** The board shall make every effort to ensure that the continuing education programs are offered either within the nurse's workplace or at another place convenient to the nurse, whether through live presentation or distance learning.

**(c) (1)** The board shall adopt rules to prescribe the methods by which the minimum standards for continuing education may be satisfied.

**(2)** The failure of any licensed nurse to satisfy the minimum standards for continuing education shall be grounds for disciplinary action or nonrenewal of the nurse's

17

license, or both.

**History:**

Acts 2001, No. 86, § 1.

## Subchapter 3 – Licensing

### § 17-87-301.  Registered Nurses

(a)  Qualifications. Before taking the examination or before the issuance of a license by endorsement, an applicant for a license to practice professional nursing shall submit to the Arkansas State Board of Nursing written evidence, verified by oath, that the applicant:

(1)  Is of good moral character;

(2)  Has completed an approved high school course of study or the equivalent thereof as determined by the appropriate educational agency; and

(3)  Has completed the required approved professional nursing education program.

(b)  Issuance of License. A license to practice as a registered nurse may be issued:

(1)  By Examination. The applicant shall be required to pass an examination in such subjects as the board may determine. Upon successfully passing the examination, the board shall issue to the applicant a license to practice professional nursing as a registered nurse;

(2)  By Endorsement. The board may issue a license to practice professional nursing as a registered nurse by endorsement to an applicant who has been duly licensed as a registered nurse under the laws of another state, territory, or foreign country if, in the opinion of the board, the applicant meets the qualifications required of registered nurses in this state at the time of graduation and if the board so recommends.

(c)  Nurses Registered Prior to March 29, 1971. Any person holding a license or certificate of registration to practice nursing as a registered nurse issued by the board which was valid on March 29, 1971, shall be deemed to be licensed as a registered nurse under the provisions of this chapter.

**(d)** Title and Abbreviation. Any person who holds a license to practice professional nursing in this state shall have the right to use the title "registered nurse" and the abbreviation "R.N.".

**History:**

Acts 1971, No. 432, § 10; 1979, No. 613, § 3; 1981 (Ex. Sess.), No. 19, §§ 1-3; A.S.A. 1947, § 72-754; Acts 1991, No. 162, § 1; 1995, No. 409, § 8.

## § 17-87-302.   Advanced Practice Nurses

**(a)**   Qualifications. In order to be licensed as an advanced practice nurse, an applicant must show evidence of education approved by the Arkansas State Board of Nursing, and national certification approved by the board under one (1) of the following:

**(1)**  Advanced Registered Nurse Practitioner. In order to qualify as an advanced registered nurse practitioner, an applicant must be currently certified as a nurse practitioner by a nationally recognized certifying body;

**(2)** Certified Registered Nurse Anesthetist. To qualify as a certified registered nurse anesthetist, an applicant must:

**(A)**   Have earned a diploma or certificate evidencing satisfactory completion, beyond generic nursing preparation, of a formal educational program that meets the standards of the Council on Accreditation of Nurse Anesthesia Educational Programs or another nationally recognized accrediting body and that has as its objective the preparation of nurses to perform as nurse anesthetists; and

**(B)**   Hold current certification from the Council on Certification of Nurse Anesthetists, the Council on Recertification of Nurse Anesthetists, or other nationally recognized certifying body;

**(3)**  Certified Nurse Midwife. To qualify as a certified nurse midwife, an applicant must:

**(A)**  Hold current certification as a nurse midwife from the American College of Nurse Midwives or other nationally recognized certifying body; and

**(B)**  Have an agreement with a consulting physician if providing intrapartum care;

**(4)**  Clinical Nurse Specialist. In order to qualify as a clinical nurse specialist, an applicant must hold a master's degree evidencing successful completion of a graduate program in nursing, which shall include supervised clinical practice and classroom instruction in a nursing specialty, and must be nationally certified in a specialty role as a clinical nurse specialist.

(b) Issuance of License. A license to practice as an advanced practice nurse may be issued:

(1) By Application. Any person holding a license to practice as a registered nurse and meeting the educational qualifications and certification requirements to be licensed as an advanced practice nurse may, upon application and payment of necessary fees to the board, be licensed as an advanced practice nurse; and

(2) By Endorsement. The board may issue a license to practice advanced practice nursing by endorsement to any applicant who has been licensed as an advanced practice nurse or to a person entitled to perform similar services under a different title under the laws of another state, territory, or foreign country if, in the opinion of the board, the applicant meets the requirements for advanced practice nurses in this state.

(c) Title and Abbreviation. Any person who holds a license to practice as an advanced practice nurse shall have the right to use the title of "advanced practice nurse" and the abbreviation "A.P.N.".

**History:**

Acts 1971, No. 432, § 2; 1979, No. 404, §§ 1, 7; 1979, No. 613, § 2; 1980 (1st Ex. Sess.), No. 14, §§ 5, 6; 1981 (Ex. Sess.), No. 19, § 8; A.S.A. 1947, §§ 72-746, 72-756.1, 72-756.2; Acts 1995, No. 409, § 9; 1999, No. 1208, § 2.

## § 17-87-303. Registered Nurse Practitioners

(a) (1) Any person holding a license to practice as a registered nurse and possessing the educational qualifications required under subsection (b) of this section to be licensed as a registered nurse practitioner may, upon application and payment of necessary fees to the Arkansas State Board of Nursing, be licensed as a registered nurse practitioner and have the right to use the title of "registered nurse practitioner" and the abbreviation "R.N.P.".

(2) No other person shall assume such a title or use such an abbreviation or any other words, letters, signs, or devices to indicate that the person using them is a registered nurse practitioner.

(b) In order to be licensed as a registered nurse practitioner, a registered nurse must hold a certificate or academic degree evidencing successful completion of the educational program of an accredited school of nursing or other nationally recognized accredited program recognized by the board as meeting the requirements of a nurse practitioner program.

**(c)** However, any person qualified to receive a license as a registered nurse practitioner may obtain the license upon the payment of a fee not to exceed twenty-five dollars ($25.00) for the original license. The license fees are to be in addition to the person's registered nurse license fees.

**History:**

Acts 1971, No. 432, §§ 2, 10; 1979, No. 404, §§ 1, 7; 1979, No. 613, §§ 2, 3; 1981 (Ex. Sess.), No. 19, §§ 1-3; A.S.A. 1947, §§ 72-746, 72-754.

## § 17-87-304. Licensed Practical Nurses

**(a)** Qualifications. An applicant for a license to practice practical nursing shall submit to the Arkansas State Board of Nursing evidence, verified by oath, that the applicant:

**(1)** Is of good moral character;

**(2)** Has completed an approved high school course of study or the equivalent thereof as determined by the appropriate educational agency; and

**(3)** Has completed a prescribed curriculum in a state-approved program for the preparation of practical nurses and holds a diploma or certificate therefrom. However, the Arkansas State Board of Nursing may waive this requirement if the board determines the applicant to be otherwise qualified.

**(b)** Issuance of License. A license to practice as a practical nurse may be issued:

**(1)** By Examination. The applicant shall be required to pass an examination in such subjects as the board may determine. Upon successful completion of the examination, the board shall issue to the applicant a license to practice as a licensed practical nurse;

**(2)** By Endorsement. The board may issue a license to practice practical nursing by endorsement to any applicant who has duly been licensed or registered as a licensed practical nurse or to a person entitled to perform similar services under a different title under the laws of another state, territory, or foreign country if, in the opinion of the board, the applicant meets the requirements for licensed practical nurses in this state at the time of graduation and if the board so recommends.

**(c)** Person Licensed Prior to March 29, 1971. Any person holding a license to practice as a practical nurse issued by the board and which was valid on March 29, 1971, shall be deemed to be licensed as a practical nurse under the provisions of this chapter.

**(d)** Title and Abbreviation. Any person who holds a license to practice practical nursing in this state shall have the right to use the title "licensed practical nurse" and the abbreviation "L.P.N.".

**History:**

Acts 1971, No. 432, § 11; 1981, No. 54, § 1; 1981 (Ex. Sess.), No. 19, §§ 4, 5; A.S.A. 1947, § 72-755; Acts 1991, No. 162, § 2; 1995, No. 409, § 10.


### § 17-87-305. Licensed Psychiatric Technician Nurses

**(a)** Qualifications. An applicant for a license to practice psychiatric technician nursing shall submit to the Arkansas State Board of Nursing evidence, verified by oath, that the applicant:

**(1)** Is of good moral character;

**(2)** Has completed an approved high school course of study or the equivalent thereof as determined by the appropriate educational agency; and

**(3)** Has completed a prescribed curriculum in a state-approved program for the preparation of psychiatric technician nurses and holds a diploma or certificate therefrom. However, the board may waive this requirement if the board determines the applicant to be otherwise qualified.

**(b)** Issuance of License. A license to practice as a psychiatric technician nurse may be issued:

**(1)** By Examination. The applicant shall be required to pass a written examination in such subjects as the board may determine. Each written examination may be supplemented by an oral examination. Upon successfully passing the examination, the board shall issue to the applicant a license to practice as a psychiatric technician nurse. All such examinations shall be conducted by an examiner, who shall be a registered nurse, and by an assistant examiner, who shall be a licensed psychiatric technician nurse;

**(2)** By Endorsement. The board may issue a license to practice psychiatric technician nursing by endorsement to an applicant who has duly been licensed or registered as a licensed psychiatric technician nurse or a person entitled to perform similar services under a different title under the laws of another state, territory, or foreign country if, in the opinion of the board, the applicant meets the requirements for licensed psychiatric technician nurses in this state at the time of graduation and if the board so recommends.

**(c)** Person Licensed Prior to March 29, 1971. Any person holding a license to practice as a psychiatric technician issued by the board in accordance with Acts 1953, No. 124 (repealed), and which was valid on March 29, 1971, shall be deemed to be licensed as a psychiatric technician nurse under the provisions of this chapter.

**(d)** Title and Abbreviation. Any person who holds a license to practice psychiatric technician nursing in this state shall have the right to use the title "licensed psychiatric technician nurse" and the abbreviation "L.P.T.N.".

**History:**

Acts 1971, No. 432, § 12; 1981, No. 54, § 2; 1981 (Ex. Sess.), No. 19, §§ 6, 7; A.S.A. 1947, § 72-756; Acts 1995, No. 409, § 11.

## § 17-87-306. Fees

The Arkansas State Board of Nursing shall establish and collect fees and penalties for services relating to certification, examination, licensing, endorsement, certification for prescriptive authority, temporary permits, license renewal, certification renewal, and other reasonable services as determined by the board.

**History:**

Acts 1995, No. 409, § 12; 2005, No. 1423, § 3.

## § 17-87-307. Temporary Permits

**(a) (1)** Upon application and payment of the required fee, the Arkansas State Board of Nursing may issue a temporary permit to practice professional, practical, or psychiatric technician nursing to a qualified applicant who has:

**(A)** Completed a program in professional, practical, or psychiatric technician nursing approved by the appropriate state or national authorizing agency of this state or country and by the appropriate authorizing agency of other states or territories or foreign countries; and

**(B)** Applied for or is awaiting results of the first examination he or she is eligible to take after the permit is issued.

**(2)** The permit shall become invalid upon notification to the applicant of the results of the first examination he or she is eligible to take after the permit is issued.

**(b) (1)** Upon application and payment of the required fee, the board shall issue a temporary permit to a qualified applicant holding a current professional, practical, or psychiatric technician license from another jurisdiction from any other state or territory awaiting endorsement.

**(2)** This permit must have an issuance date and an expiration date. The permit shall be valid for no more than six (6) months.

**(c) (1)** Upon application and payment of the required fee, an applicant shall be issued a temporary permit to practice advanced practice nursing who has:

**(A)** Satisfactorily completed an educational program for advanced practice nursing approved by the board; and

**(B)** Been accepted by the appropriate certification body to sit for the first national certification exam he or she is eligible to take.

**(2)** The permit shall expire upon notification to the applicant of the results of the examination.

**(3)** The permit is not renewable and does not apply to prescriptive authority.

**(d) (1)** Upon application and payment of the required fee, the board shall issue a temporary permit to a qualified applicant holding a current advanced practice nurse license or the equivalent from another jurisdiction from any other state or territory awaiting endorsement.

**(2) (A)** This permit must have an issuance date and a date when it shall become invalid.

**(B)** The permit shall automatically become invalid upon notification of the applicant's failure to pass the appropriate national certification exam.

**(C)** In no event shall the permit be valid in excess of six (6) months.

**History:**

Acts 1971, No. 432, § 13; 1977, No. 88, § 1; 1979, No. 90, § 1; 1980 (1st Ex. Sess.), No. 14, § 2; 1981 (Ex. Sess.), No. 19, § 9; A.S.A. 1947, § 72-757; Acts 1995, No. 409, § 13; 2001, No. 303, § 1

## § 17-87-308.  Renewal of Licenses

**(a) (1)** The Arkansas State Board of Nursing shall prescribe the procedure for the cyclical biennial renewal of licenses to every person licensed by the board.

**(2)** In each case, the board shall mail a notification for renewal to the licensee at least thirty (30) days prior to the expiration date of the license.

**(b)** Upon receipt of the application and the fee, the board shall verify the accuracy of the application and renew the license for a period to expire on the last day of the current biennial cycle.

**(c)** The renewal shall render the holder a legal practitioner of nursing for the period stated in subsection (b) of this section.

**(d)** Any licensee who allows his or her license to lapse by failing to renew the license as provided in this section may be reinstated by the board on payment of the renewal fee plus a penalty.

**(e)** Any person practicing nursing during the time his or her license has lapsed shall be considered an illegal practitioner and shall be subject to the penalties provided for violations of this chapter.

**(f) (1) (A)** An individual may place his or her license on inactive status with written notification to the board.

**(B)** The holder of an inactive license shall not practice nursing in this state.

**(2) (A)** The provisions relating to the denial, suspension, and revocation of a license shall be applicable to an inactive or lapsed license.

**(B)** When proceedings to suspend or revoke an inactive license or otherwise discipline the holder of an inactive license have been initiated, the license shall not be reinstated until the proceedings have been completed.

**(3)** An inactive license may be placed in an active status upon compliance with the rules established by the board.

**(g)** As a condition of licensure renewal, an advanced practice nurse shall submit proof of current national certification and successful completion of continuing education as required by the board.

**History:**

Acts 1971, No. 432, § 13; 1981 (Ex. Sess.), No. 19, § 9; A.S.A. 1947, § 72-

757; Acts 1987, No. 147, § 1; 1995, No. 409, § 14; 1997, No. 179, § 14; 2005, No. 61,

## § 17-87-309. Disciplinary Actions

(a) The Arkansas State Board of Nursing shall have sole authority to deny, suspend, revoke, or limit any license or privilege to practice nursing or certificate of prescriptive authority issued by the board or applied for in accordance with the provisions of this chapter or to otherwise discipline a licensee upon proof that the person:

(1) Is guilty of fraud or deceit in procuring or attempting to procure a license to practice nursing or is engaged in the practice of nursing without a valid license;

(2) Is guilty of a crime or gross immorality;

(3) Is unfit or incompetent by reason of negligence, habits, or other causes;

(4) Is habitually intemperate or is addicted to the use of habit-forming drugs;

(5) Is mentally incompetent;

(6) Is guilty of unprofessional conduct;

(7) Has had a license, privilege to practice, certificate, or registration revoked or suspended or has been placed on probation or under disciplinary order in any jurisdiction;

(8) Has voluntarily surrendered a license, privilege to practice, certification, or registration and has not been reinstated in any jurisdiction; or

(9) Has willfully or repeatedly violated any of the provisions of this chapter.

(b) The board shall refuse to issue or shall revoke the license of any person who is found guilty of or pleads guilty or nolo contendere to any offense listed in § 17-87-312(f), unless the person requests and the board grants a waiver pursuant to § 17-87-312(h).

(c) Proceedings under this section shall be as provided in the Arkansas Administrative Procedure Act, § 25-15-201 et seq.

**History:**

Acts 1971, No. 432, § 16; A.S.A. 1947, § 72-760; Acts 1995, No. 409, § 15; 1999, No. 1208, § 3; 2001, No. 212, § 1; 2007, No. 207, § 1.

## § 17-87-310. Prescriptive Authority

(a) The Arkansas State Board of Nursing may grant a certificate of prescriptive authority to an advanced practice nurse who:

(1) Submits proof of successful completion of a board-approved advanced pharmacology course that shall include preceptorial experience in the prescription of drugs, medicines, and therapeutic devices; and

(2) Has a collaborative practice agreement with a physician who is licensed under the Arkansas Medical Practices Act, §§ 17-95-201–17-95-207, 17-95-301–17-95-305, and 17-95-401–17-95-411, and who has a practice comparable in scope, specialty, or expertise to that of the advanced practice nurse on file with the board.

(b) (1) An advanced practice nurse with a certificate of prescriptive authority may receive and prescribe drugs, medicines, or therapeutic devices appropriate to the advanced practice nurse's area of practice in accordance with rules established by the board.

(2) An advanced practice nurse's prescriptive authority shall only extend to drugs listed in Schedules III–V.

(c) A collaborative practice agreement shall include, but not be limited to, provisions addressing:

(1) The availability of the collaborating physician for consultation or referral, or both;

(2) Methods of management of the collaborative practice, which shall include protocols for prescriptive authority;

(3) Coverage of the health care needs of a patient in the emergency absence of the advanced practice nurse or physician; and

(4) Quality assurance.

(d) If a collaborative practice results in complaints of violations of the Arkansas Medical Practices Act, §§ 17-95-201–17-95-207, 17-95-301–17-95-305, and 17-95-401–17-95-411, the Arkansas State Medical Board may review the role of the physician in the collaborative practice to determine if the physician is unable to manage his or her responsibilities under the agreement without an adverse affect on the quality of care of the patient.

(e) If a collaborative practice results in complaints of violations of this chapter, the Arkansas State Board of Nursing may review the role of the advanced practice nurse in the collaborative practice to determine if the nurse is unable to manage his or her responsibilities under the agreement without an adverse affect on the quality of care of the patient.

**History:**

    Acts 1995, No. 409, § 16.

## § 17-87-311.  Direct Reimbursement Agreements

    **(a)** An advanced practice nurse or a registered nurse practitioner may enter into a direct reimbursement agreement with the agency administering the state medicaid program.

    **(b)** The agency administering the state medicaid program shall not discriminate against practitioners providing covered services within the scope of their practice based on the type of practitioner.

**History:**

    Acts 1995, No. 409, § 17.

## § 17-87-312.  Criminal Background Checks

    **(a)** Each first-time applicant for a license issued by the Arkansas State Board of Nursing shall apply to the Identification Bureau of the Department of Arkansas State Police for a state and national criminal background check, to be conducted by the Federal Bureau of Investigation.

    **(b)** The check shall conform to the applicable federal standards and shall include the taking of fingerprints.

    **(c)** The applicant shall sign a release of information to the board and shall be responsible to the Department of Arkansas State Police for the payment of any fee associated with the criminal background check.

    **(d)** Upon completion of the criminal background check, the Identification Bureau of the Department of Arkansas State Police shall forward to the board all information obtained concerning the applicant in the commission of any offense listed in subsection (e) of this section.

**(e)** Except as provided in subdivision (l)(1) of this section, no person shall be eligible to receive or hold a license issued by the board if that person has pleaded guilty or nolo contendere to or has been found guilty of any of the following offenses by any court in the State of Arkansas or of any similar offense by a court in another state or of any similar offense by a federal court:

**(1)** Capital murder as prohibited in § 5-10-101;

**(2)** Murder in the first degree as prohibited in § 5-10-102 and murder in the second degree as prohibited in § 5-10-103;

**(3)** Manslaughter as prohibited in § 5-10-104;

**(4)** Negligent homicide as prohibited in § 5-10-105;

**(5)** Kidnaping as prohibited in § 5-11-102;

**(6)** False imprisonment in the first degree as prohibited in § 5-11-103;

**(7)** Permanent detention or restraint as prohibited in § 5-11-106;

**(8)** Robbery as prohibited in § 5-12-102;

**(9)** Aggravated robbery as prohibited in § 5-12-103;

**(10)** Battery in the first degree as prohibited in § 5-13-201;

**(11)** Aggravated assault as prohibited in § 5-13-204;

**(12)** Introduction of a controlled substance into the body of another person as prohibited in § 5-13-210;

**(13)** Terroristic threatening in the first degree as prohibited in § 5-13-301;

**(14)** Rape as prohibited in § 5-14-103;

**(15)** Sexual indecency with a child as prohibited in § 5-14-110;

**(16)** Sexual assault in the first degree, second degree, third degree, and fourth degree as prohibited in §§ 5-14-124 — 5-14-127;

**(17)** Incest as prohibited in § 5-26-202;

**(18)** Offenses against the family as prohibited in §§ 5-26-303–5-26-306;

**(19)** Endangering the welfare of an incompetent person in the first degree as prohibited in § 5-27-201;

     **(20)** Endangering the welfare of a minor in the first degree as prohibited in § 5-27-205;

     **(21)** Permitting abuse of a minor as prohibited in § 5-27-221(a)(1) and (3);

     **(22)** Engaging children in sexually explicit conduct for use in visual or print media, transportation of minors for prohibited sexual conduct, pandering or possessing visual or print medium depicting sexually explicit conduct involving a child, or use of a child or consent to use of a child in a sexual performance by producing, directing, or promoting a sexual performance by a child as prohibited in §§ 5-27-303–5-27-305, 5-27-402, and 5-27-403;

     **(23)** Felony adult abuse as prohibited in § 5-28-103;

     **(24)** Theft of property as prohibited in § 5-36-103;

     **(25)** Theft by receiving as prohibited in § 5-36-106;

     **(26)** Arson as prohibited in § 5-38-301;

     **(27)** Burglary as prohibited in § 5-39-201;

     **(28)** Felony violation of the Uniform Controlled Substances Act, §§ 5-64-101–5-64-608 as prohibited in § 5-64-401;

     **(29)** Promotion of prostitution in the first degree as prohibited in § 5-70-104;

     **(30)** Stalking as prohibited in § 5-71-229;

     **(31)** Criminal attempt, criminal complicity, criminal solicitation, or criminal conspiracy as prohibited in §§ 5-3-201, 5-3-202, 5-3-301, and 5-3-401, to commit any of the offenses listed in this subsection;

     **(32)** Computer child pornography as prohibited in § 5-27-603; and

     **(33)** Computer exploitation of a child in the first degree as prohibited in § 5-27-605.

     **(f) (1) (A)** The board may issue a nonrenewable temporary permit for licensure to a first-time applicant pending the results of the criminal background check.

     **(B)** The permit shall be valid for no more than six (6) months.

     **(2)** Except as provided in subdivision (l)(1) of this section, upon receipt of information from the Identification Bureau of the Department of Arkansas State Police that the person holding the letter of provisional licensure has pleaded guilty or nolo contendere to, or has been found guilty of, any offense listed in subsection (e) of this section, the board shall immediately revoke the provisional license.

(g) (1) The provisions of subsection (e) and subdivision (f)(2) of this section may be waived by the board upon the request of:

(A) An affected applicant for licensure; or

(B) The person holding a license subject to revocation.

(2) Circumstances for which a waiver may be granted shall include, but not be limited to, the following:

(A) The age at which the crime was committed;

(B) The circumstances surrounding the crime;

(C) The length of time since the crime;

(D) Subsequent work history;

(E) Employment references;

(F) Character references; and

(G) Other evidence demonstrating that the applicant does not pose a threat to the health or safety of the public.

(h) (1) Any information received by the board from the Identification Bureau of the Department of Arkansas State Police pursuant to this section shall not be available for examination except by:

(A) The affected applicant for licensure or his or her authorized representative; or

(B) The person whose license is subject to revocation or his or her authorized representative.

(2) No record, file, or document shall be removed from the custody of the Department of Arkansas State Police.

(i) Any information made available to the affected applicant for licensure or the person whose license is subject to revocation shall be information pertaining to that person only.

(j) Rights of privilege and confidentiality established in this section shall not extend to any document created for purposes other than this background check.

**(k)** The board shall adopt the necessary rules and regulations to fully implement the provisions of this section.

**(l) (1)** For purposes of this section, an expunged record of a conviction or a plea of guilty or nolo contendere to an offense listed in subsection (e) of this section shall not be considered a conviction, guilty plea, or nolo contendere plea to the offense unless the offense is also listed in subdivision (l)(2) of this section.

**(2)** Because of the serious nature of the offenses and the close relationship to the type of work that is to be performed, the following shall result in permanent disqualification:

**(A)** Capital murder as prohibited in § 5-10-101;

**(B)** Murder in the first degree as prohibited in § 5-10-102 and murder in the second degree as prohibited in § 5-10-103;

**(C)** Kidnaping as prohibited in § 5-11-102;

**(D)** Rape as prohibited in § 5-14-103;

**(E)** Sexual assault in the first degree as prohibited in § 5-14-124 and sexual assault in the second degree as prohibited in § 5-14-125;

**(F)** Endangering the welfare of a minor in the first degree as prohibited in § 5-27-205 and endangering the welfare of a minor in the second degree as prohibited in § 5-27-206;

**(G)** Incest as prohibited in § 5-26-202;

**(H)** Arson as prohibited in § 5-38-301;

**(I)** Endangering the welfare of an incompetent person in the first degree as prohibited in § 5-27-201; and

**(J)** Adult abuse that constitutes a felony as prohibited in § 5-28-103.

**History:**

Acts 1999, No. 1208, § 4; 2001, No. 303, §§ 2-4; 2003, No. 103, §§ 1, 2; No. 1087, § 15; No. 1386, § 1; No. 1449, § 1; 2005, No. 1923, § 2.

## Subchapter 4 – Educational Programs

### § 17-87-401. Nursing Education Programs

(a) An institution desiring to conduct a nursing education program to prepare professional, advanced practice, nurse practitioner, practical, and psychiatric technician nurses shall apply to the Arkansas State Board of Nursing and submit evidence that:

(1) It is prepared to carry out a program in professional nursing education, advanced practice nursing education, nurse practitioner nursing education, practical nursing education, or psychiatric technician nursing training, as the case may be; and

(2) It is prepared to meet such standards as shall be established by this chapter and by the board.

(b) (1) A survey of the institution and its entire nursing education program shall be made by an authorized representative of the board, who shall submit a written report of the survey to the board.

(2) If, in the opinion of the board, the requirements for an approved nursing education program are met, the program shall be approved as a nursing education program for professional, advanced practice, nurse practitioner, practical, and psychiatric technician nurses.

(c) (1) From time to time, as deemed necessary, it shall be the duty of the board, through its authorized representative, to survey its nursing education programs in the state.

(2) Written reports of such surveys shall be submitted to the board.

(3) If the board shall determine that any approved nursing education program under its supervision is not maintaining the standards required by the statutes and by the board, notice thereof in writing specifying the defect or defects shall be immediately given to the institution conducting the program.

(4) A program which fails within a reasonable time to correct these conditions to the satisfaction of the board shall be withdrawn after a hearing.

**History:**

Acts 1971, No. 432, § 15; A.S.A. 1947, § 72-759; Acts 1995, No. 409, § 18.

### § 17-87-402.  Institutions of Higher Education-Challenge and Validation Examinations

**(a)** As used in this section, unless the context otherwise requires:

**(1)** "Challenge examination" means a test designed to determine the level of knowledge of the person being tested in the subject area of the test. Challenge examinations may cover any area of academic pursuit; and

**(2)** "Validation examination" means an evaluation of prior knowledge, experience, or skills. Validation examinations are administered to determine the proper placement of the examinee within the nurse training program.

**(b)** The Department of Higher Education shall:

**(1)** Encourage and supervise the development of methods of validation of nursing knowledge and skills through written and clinical testing mechanisms;

**(2)** Review and approve validation and challenge examinations for fairness and relevant content;

**(3)** Set uniform passing scores to be used by institutions of higher education in this state for passing standardized validation and challenge examinations when the passing scores are not determined at the national level; and

**(4)** Require schools using individual school-made tests to select one (1) standard passing score for each test which any level of student must achieve to receive credit.

**(c)** All institutions of higher education in this state shall use standardized validation and challenge examinations or devise their own. All challenge examinations and all validation examinations shall be submitted to the Department of Higher Education for its approval. Upon the successful passing of a validation examination or challenge examination, the examinee shall be given credit for the course which is the subject of the test.

**(d)** Each Arkansas institution of higher education shall accept the credit given by other Arkansas institutions of higher education for the successful passing of a challenge examination or a validation examination on any course required in the nursing curriculum.

**(e) (1)** Licensed practical nurses and licensed psychiatric technician nurses may transfer or challenge by test, or validate, up to thirty (30) semester credit hours from the total nursing program curriculum upon entering diploma, associate degree, or baccalaureate degree programs in nursing in Arkansas. This does not include other hours they may have earned which may also be transferred.

**(2)** Registered nurses may transfer or challenge by test, or validate, up to sixty (60) semester credit hours from the total nursing program curriculum upon entering a baccalaureate degree program in nursing in Arkansas. This does not include other hours they may have earned which may also be transferred.

**History:**

Acts 1979, No. 88, §§ 1-5; A.S.A. 1947, §§ 72-759.1–72-759.5.

## § 17-87-403. Nursing Recruitment and Admission

Upon request, the Arkansas State Board of Nursing shall provide assistance to publicly supported institutions of higher education in implementing programs offered under § 6-60-212.

**History:**

Acts 2005, No. 1256, § 2.

## Subchapter 5 – Nurse Midwives Section

§§ 17-87-501–17-87-507. [Repealed.]

## Subchapter 6 – Nurse Licensure Compact

## § 17-87-601.  Text of Compact

The Interstate Nurse Licensure Compact is enacted into law and entered into by this state with all states legally joining therein and in the form substantially as follows:

## NURSE LICENSURE COMPACT[1]

## ARTICLE I
## FINDINGS AND DECLARATION OF PURPOSE

(a) The party states find that:

(1) The health and safety of the public are affected by the degree of compliance with and the effectiveness of enforcement activities related to state nurse licensure laws;

(2) Violations of nurse licensure and other laws regulating the practice of nursing may result in injury or harm to the public;

(3) The expanded mobility of nurses and the use of advanced communication technologies as part of our nation's healthcare delivery system require greater coordination and cooperation among states in the areas of nurse licensure and regulation;

(4) New practice modalities and technology make compliance with individual state nurse licensure laws difficult and complex; and

(5) The current system of duplicative licensure for nurses practicing in multiple states is cumbersome and redundant to both nurses and states.

(b) The general purposes of this Compact are to:

(1) Facilitate the states' responsibility to protect the public's health and safety;

(2) Ensure and encourage the cooperation of party states in the areas of nurse licensure and regulation;

---

[1]  Note: 24 states are a party to this Compact, including Arkansas. http://www.ncsbn.org/nlc.htm. (footnote added)

**(3)** Facilitate the exchange of information between party states in the areas of nurse regulation, investigation, and adverse actions;

**(4)** Promote compliance with the laws governing the practice of nursing in each jurisdiction;

**(5)** Invest all party states with the authority to hold a nurse accountable for meeting all state practice laws in the state in which the patient is located at the time care is rendered through the mutual recognition of party state licenses.

## ARTICLE II
## DEFINITIONS

As used in this Compact:

**(1)** "Adverse action" means a home or remote state action;

**(2)** "Alternative program" means a voluntary, nondisciplinary monitoring program approved by a nurse licensing board;

**(3)** "Coordinated Licensure Information System" means an integrated process for collecting, storing, and sharing information on nurse licensure and enforcement activities related to nurse licensure laws, which is administered by a non-profit organization composed of and controlled by state nurse licensing boards;

**(4)** "Current significant investigative information" means:

**(A)** Investigative information that a licensing board after a preliminary inquiry that includes notification and an opportunity for the nurse to respond if required by state law, has reason to believe is not groundless and, if proved true, would indicate more than a minor infraction; or

**(B)** Investigative information that indicates that the nurse represents an immediate threat to public health and safety regardless of whether the nurse has been notified and had an opportunity to respond;

**(5)** "Home state" means the party state which is the nurse's primary state of residence;

**(6)** "Home state action" means any administrative, civil, equitable or criminal action permitted by the home state's laws which are imposed on a nurse by the home state's licensing board or other authority including actions against an individual's license such as: revocation, suspension, probation, or any other action which affects a nurse's authorization to practice;

**(7)** "Licensing board" means a party state's regulatory body responsible for issuing nurse licenses;

**(8)** "Multistate licensure privilege" means current, official authority from a remote state permitting the practice of nursing as either a registered nurse or a licensed practical/vocational nurse in such party state. All party states have the authority, in accordance with existing state due process law, to take actions against the nurse's privilege such as: revocation, suspension, probation, or any other action which affects a nurse's authorization to practice;

**(9)** "Nurse" means a registered nurse or licensed practical/vocational nurse, as those terms are defined by each party's state practice laws;

**(10)** "Party state" means any state that has adopted this Compact;

**(11)** "Remote state" means a party state, other than the home state:

**(A)** Where the patient is located at the time nursing care is provided; or

**(B)** In the case of the practice of nursing not involving a patient, in such party state where the recipient of nursing practice is located;

**(12)** "Remote state action" means:

**(A)** Any administrative, civil, equitable, or criminal action permitted by a remote state's laws which are imposed on a nurse by the remote state's licensing board or other authority including actions against an individual's multistate licensure privilege to practice in the remote state; and

**(B)** Cease and desist and other injunctive or equitable orders issued by remote states or the licensing boards thereof;

**(13)** "State" means a state, territory, or possession of the United States, the District of Columbia, or the Commonwealth of Puerto Rico; and

**(14)** "State practice laws" means those individual party's state laws and regulations that govern the practice of nursing, define the scope of nursing practice, and create the methods and grounds for imposing discipline. "State practice laws" does not include the initial qualifications for licensure or requirements necessary to obtain and retain a license, except for qualifications or requirements of the home state.

# ARTICLE III

## GENERAL PROVISIONS AND JURISDICTION

**(a)** A license to practice registered nursing issued by a home state to a resident in that state will be recognized by each party state as authorizing a multistate licensure privilege to practice as a registered nurse in such party state. A license to practice licensed practical/vocational nursing issued by a home state to a resident in that state will be recognized by each party state as authorizing a multistate licensure privilege to practice as a licensed practical/vocational nurse in such party state. In order to obtain or retain a license, an applicant must meet the home state's qualifications for licensure and license renewal as well as all other applicable state laws.

**(b)** Party states may, in accordance with state due process laws, limit or revoke the multistate licensure privilege of any nurse to practice in their states and may take any other actions under their applicable state laws necessary to protect the health and safety of their citizens. If a party state takes such action, it shall promptly notify the administrator of the coordinated licensure information system. The administrator of the coordinated licensure information system shall promptly notify the home state of any such actions by remote states.

**(c)** Every nurse practicing in a party state must comply with the state practice laws of the state in which the patient is located at the time care is rendered. In addition, the practice of nursing is not limited to patient care, but shall include all nursing practice as defined by the state practice laws of a party state. The practice of nursing will subject a nurse to the jurisdiction of the nurse licensing board and the courts, as well as the laws, in that party state.

**(d)** This Compact does not affect additional requirements imposed by states for advanced practice registered nursing. However, a multistate licensure privilege to practice registered nursing granted by a party state shall be recognized by other party states as a license to practice registered nursing if one is required by state law as a precondition for qualifying for advanced practice registered nurse authorization.

**(e)** Individuals not residing in a party state shall continue to be able to apply for nurse licensure as provided for under the laws of each party state. However, the license granted to these individuals will not be recognized as granting the privilege to practice nursing in any other party state unless explicitly agreed to by that party state.

# ARTICLE IV
## APPLICATIONS FOR LICENSURE IN A PARTY STATE

**(a)** Upon application for a license, the licensing board in a party state shall ascertain, through the coordinated licensure information system, whether the applicant has ever held, or is the holder of, a license issued by any other state, whether there are any restrictions on the multistate licensure privilege, and whether any other adverse action by any state has been taken against the license.

**(b)** A nurse in a party state shall hold licensure in only one (1) party state at a time, issued by the home state.

**(c)** A nurse who intends to change primary state of residence may apply for licensure in the new home state in advance of such change. However, new licenses will not be issued by a party state until after a nurse provides evidence of change in primary state of residence satisfactory to the new home state's licensing board.

**(d)** When a nurse changes primary state of residence by:

**(1)** Moving between two party states, and obtains a license from the new home state, the license from the former home state is no longer valid;

**(2)** Moving from a nonparty state to a party state, and obtains a license from the new home state, the individual state license issued by the nonparty state is not affected and will remain in full force if so provided by the laws of the nonparty state;

**(3)** Moving from a party state to a nonparty state, the license issued by the prior home state converts to an individual state license, valid only in the former home state, without the multistate licensure privilege to practice in other party states.

# ARTICLE V
## ADVERSE ACTIONS

In addition to the General Provisions described in Article III, the following provisions apply:

**(1)** The licensing board of a remote state shall promptly report to the administrator of the coordinated licensure information system any remote state actions including the factual and legal basis for such action, if known. The licensing board of a remote state shall also promptly report any significant current investigative information yet to result in a remote state action. The administrator of the coordinated licensure information system shall promptly notify the home state of any such reports;

**(2)** The licensing board of a party state shall have the authority to complete any pending investigations for a nurse who changes primary state of residence during the course of such investigations. It shall also have the authority to take appropriate action(s), and shall promptly report the conclusions of such investigations to the administrator of the coordinated licensure information system. The administrator of the coordinated licensure information system shall promptly notify the new home state of any such actions;

**(3)** A remote state may take adverse action affecting the multistate licensure privilege to practice within that party state. However, only the home state shall have the power to impose adverse action against the license issued by the home state;

**(4)** For purposes of imposing adverse action, the licensing board of the home state shall give the same priority and effect to reported conduct received from a remote state as it would if such conduct had occurred within the home state. In so doing, it shall apply its own state laws to determine appropriate action;

**(5)** The home state may take adverse action based on the factual findings of the remote state, so long as each state follows its own procedures for imposing such adverse action; and

**(6)** Nothing in this Compact shall override a party state's decision that participation in an alternative program may be used in lieu of licensure action and that such participation shall remain nonpublic if required by the party state's laws. Party states must require nurses who enter any alternative programs to agree not to practice in any other party state during the term of the alternative program without prior authorization from such other party state.

## ARTICLE VI
## ADDITIONAL AUTHORITIES INVESTED IN PARTY
## STATE NURSE LICENSING BOARDS

Notwithstanding any other powers, party state nurse licensing boards shall have the authority to:

**(1)** If otherwise permitted by state law, recover from the affected nurse the costs of investigations and disposition of cases resulting from any adverse action taken against that nurse;

**(2)** Issue subpoenas for both hearings and investigations which require the attendance and testimony of witnesses, and the production of evidence. Subpoenas issued by a nurse licensing board in a party state for the attendance and testimony of witnesses, and/or the production of evidence from another party state, shall be enforced in the latter state by any

41

court of competent jurisdiction, according to the practice and procedure of that court applicable to subpoenas issued in proceedings pending before it. The issuing authority shall pay any witness fees, travel expenses, mileage and other fees required by the service statutes of the state where the witnesses and/or evidence are located;

**(3)** Issue cease and desist orders to limit or revoke a nurse's authority to practice in their state; and

**(4)** Promulgate uniform rules and regulations as provided for in Article VIII(c).

# ARTICLE VII
## COORDINATED LICENSURE INFORMATION SYSTEM

**(a)** All party states shall participate in a cooperative effort to create a coordinated database of all licensed registered nurses and licensed practical/vocational nurses. This system will include information on the licensure and disciplinary history of each nurse, as contributed by party states, to assist in the coordination of nurse licensure and enforcement efforts.

**(b)** Notwithstanding any other provision of law, all party states' licensing boards shall promptly report adverse actions, actions against multistate licensure privileges, any current significant investigative information yet to result in adverse action, denials of applications, and the reasons for such denials, to the coordinated licensure information system.

**(c)** Current significant investigative information shall be transmitted through the coordinated licensure information system only to party state licensing boards.

**(d)** Notwithstanding any other provision of law, all party states' licensing boards contributing information to the coordinated licensure information system may designate information that may not be shared with nonparty states or disclosed to other entities or individuals without the express permission of the contributing state.

**(e)** Any personally identifiable information obtained by a party states' licensing board from the coordinated licensure information system may not be shared with nonparty states or disclosed to other entities or individuals except to the extent permitted by the laws of the party state contributing the information.

**(f)** Any information contributed to the coordinated licensure information system that is subsequently required to be expunged by the laws of the party states contributing that information, shall also be expunged from the coordinated licensure information system.

**(g)** The compact administrators, acting jointly with each other and in consultation

42

with the administrator of the coordinated licensure information system, shall formulate necessary and proper procedures for the identification, collection, and exchange of information under this Compact.

## ARTICLE VIII
## COMPACT ADMINISTRATION AND INTERCHANGE OF INFORMATION

**(a)** The head of the nurse licensing board, or his/her designee, of each party state shall be the administrator of this Compact for his/her state.

**(b)** The compact administrator of each party state shall furnish to the compact administrator of each other party state any information and documents including, but not limited to, a uniform data set of investigations, identifying information, licensure data, and disclosable alternative program participation information to facilitate the administration of this Compact.

**(c)** Compact administrators shall have the authority to develop uniform rules to facilitate and coordinate implementation of this Compact. These uniform rules shall be adopted by party states, under the authority invested under Article VI(d).

## ARTICLE IX
## IMMUNITY

No party state or the officers or employees or agents of a party state's nurse licensing board who acts in accordance with the provisions of this Compact shall be liable on account of any act or omission in good faith while engaged in the performance of their duties under this Compact. Good faith in this article shall not include willful misconduct or gross negligence.

## ARTICLE X
## ENTRY INTO FORCE, WITHDRAWAL AND AMENDMENT

**(a)** This Compact shall enter into force and become effective as to any state when it has been enacted into the laws of that state. Any party state may withdraw from this Compact by enacting a statute repealing the same, but no such withdrawal shall take effect until six (6) months after the withdrawing state has given notice of the withdrawal to the executive heads of all other party states.

**(b)** No withdrawal shall affect the validity or applicability by the licensing boards of states remaining party to the Compact of any report of adverse action occurring prior to the withdrawal.

**(c)** Nothing contained in this Compact shall be construed to invalidate or prevent any nurse licensure agreement or other cooperative arrangement between a party state and a nonparty state that is made in accordance with the other provisions of this Compact.

**(d)** This Compact may be amended by the party states. No amendment to this Compact shall become effective and binding upon the party states unless and until it is enacted into the laws of all party states.

## ARTICLE XI
## CONSTRUCTION AND SEVERABILITY

**(a)** This Compact shall be liberally construed so as to effectuate the purposes thereof. The provisions of this Compact shall be severable and if any phrase, clause, sentence, or provision of this Compact is declared to be contrary to the constitution of any party state or of the United States or the applicability thereof to any government, agency, person, or circumstance is held invalid, the validity of the remainder of this Compact and the applicability thereof to any government, agency, person, or circumstance shall not be affected thereby. If this Compact shall be held contrary to the constitution of any state party thereto, the Compact shall remain in full force and effect as to the remaining party states and in full force and effect as to the party state affected as to all severable matters.

**(b)** In the event party states find a need for settling disputes arising under this Compact:

**(1)** The party states may submit the issues in dispute to an arbitration panel which will be comprised of an individual appointed by the compact administrator in the home state; an individual appointed by the compact administrator in the remote state(s) involved; and an individual mutually agreed upon by the compact administrators of all the party states involved in the dispute; and

**(2)** The decision of a majority of the arbitrators shall be final and binding.

## § 17-87-602.  Practice Privileges – Power of Board to Limit or Revoke

The Arkansas State Board of Nursing may limit or revoke practice privileges in this state of a person licensed to practice nursing by a jurisdiction that has joined the Compact or take action on previous practice privilege action from another party state.

**History:**

Acts 1999, No. 220, § 2.

## § 17-87-603.  Definition

For purposes of this subchapter, the term "head of the nurse licensing board" shall mean the Executive Director of the Arkansas State Board of Nursing.

**History:**

Acts 1999, No. 220, § 3.

## § 17-87-604.  Effective Date

**(a)** The effective date of this Compact shall be July 1, 2000.

**(b)** Upon the effective date of this compact, the licensing board shall participate in an evaluation of the effectiveness and operability of the compact. Upon completion of the evaluation, a report shall be submitted to the Legislative Council for its review.

**History:**

Acts 1999, No. 220, § 4.

## Subchapter 7 – Medication Assistive Persons

### § 17-87-701.  Definitions

As used in this subchapter:

**(1)** "Board" means the Arkansas State Board of Nursing;

**(2)** "Designated facility" means a type of facility determined by the board as an environment in which medication assistive persons may serve in accordance with the requirements of this subchapter and regulations promulgated by the board;

**(3)** "Medication assistive person" means a person who is certified by the board to administer certain nonprescription and legend drugs in designated facilities; and

**(4)** "Supervision" means the active oversight of patient care services while on the premises of a designated facility in a manner defined by the board.

**History:**

Acts 2005, No. 1423, § 4.

### § 17-87-702.  Certificate Required.

In order to safeguard life and health, any person serving or offering to serve as a medication assistive person shall:

**(1)** Submit evidence that he or she is qualified to so serve; and

**(2)** Be certified as provided in this subchapter.

**History:**

Acts 2005, No. 1423, § 4.

### § 17-87-703.  Designated Facilities.

**(a)** The Arkansas State Board of Nursing shall designate the types of facilities that may use medication assistive persons.

**(b) (1)** Designated facilities may not be required to use medication assistive persons.

**(2)** However, if a designated facility elects to use medication assistive personnel, the facility shall notify the board in a manner prescribed by the board.

**History:**

Acts 2005, No. 1423, § 4.

## § 17-87-704.  Qualifications

**(a)** In order to be certified as a medication assistive person, an applicant shall submit to the Arkansas State Board of Nursing written evidence, verified by oath, that the applicant:

**(1) (A)** Is currently listed in good standing on the state's certified nurse aide registry;

**(B)** Has maintained registration on the state's certified nurse aide registry continuously for a minimum of one (1) year;

**(C)** Has completed at least one (1) continuous year of full-time experience as a certified nurse aide in this state;

**(D)** Is currently employed at a designated facility;

**(E)** Has a high school diploma or the equivalent;

**(F)** Has successfully completed a literacy and reading comprehension screening process approved by the board;

**(G)** Has successfully completed a medication assistive person training course of not less than one hundred (100) hours approved by the board; and

**(H)** Has successfully passed an examination on subjects the board determines; or

**(2) (A)** Has completed a portion of a nursing education program equivalent to the medication assistive person training course; and

**(B)** Passed the medication aide examination.

**(b)** The board may issue a certification as a medication assistive person by endorsement to an applicant who has been licensed or certified as a medication assistive person under the laws of another state or territory, if:

**(1)** In the opinion of the board, the applicant meets the qualifications of medication assistive persons in this state; and

**(2)** The board recommends certification.

**(c)** Any person holding a certification as a medication assistive person shall have the right to use the title "medication assistive person" and the abbreviation "M.A.P.".

**History:**

Acts 2005, No. 1423, § 4; 2007, No. 206, § 1.

### § 17-87-705.  Scope of Work

**(a) (1)** A medication assistive person may perform the delegated nursing function of medication administration and related tasks in accordance with rules promulgated by the Arkansas State Board of Nursing.

**(2)** A medication assistive person shall perform medication administration and related tasks only:

**(A)** At a designated facility; and

**(B)** Under the supervision of a licensed nurse.

**(3) (A)** Medication administration shall be limited to the administration of nonprescription and legend drugs ordered by an authorized prescriber by the following methods:

**(i)** Orally;

**(ii)** Topically;

**(iii)** Drops for eye, ear, or nose;

**(iv)** Vaginally;

**(v)** Rectally;

**(vi)** Transdermally; and

**(vii)** Via oral inhaler.

**(B)** Medication administration by a medication assistive person shall not include controlled substances.

**(b)** A medication assistive person shall not:

**(1)** Receive, have access to, or administer any controlled substance;

**(2)** Administer parenteral, enteral, or injectable medications;

**(3)** Administer any substances by nasogastric or gastrostomy tubes;

**(4)** Calculate drug dosages;

**(5)** Destroy medication;

**(6)** Receive orders, either in writing or verbally, for new or changed medications;

**(7)** Transcribe orders from the medical record;

**(8)** Order initial medications;

**(9)** Evaluate medication error reports;

**(10)** Perform treatments;

**(11)** Conduct patient assessments or evaluations; or

**(12)** Engage in patient teaching activities.

**History:** Acts 2005, No. 1423, § 4.

### § 17-87-706.  Renewal of Certifications

**(a) (1)** The Arkansas State Board of Nursing shall prescribe the procedure for the cyclical renewal of medication assistive person certifications.

**(2)** In each case, the board shall mail a notification for renewal to the medication assistive person at least thirty (30) days before the expiration date of the certification.

**(b) (1)** Upon receipt of the renewal application and the fee, the board shall verify the accuracy of the application.

**(2) (A)** If the board finds the application to be accurate, the board shall issue a certificate of renewal to the applicant.

**(B)** As a condition of certification renewal, a medication assistive person shall be:

**(i)** Currently listed in good standing on the state's certified nurse aide registry; and

**(ii)** Required to satisfactorily complete at least eight (8) hours of continuing medication education course work as required by the board.

**(c)** The renewal shall render the holder of the certificate a legal provider of medication assistive person services for the period stated in the certificate of renewal.

**(d)** Any medication assistive person who allows his or her certification to lapse by failing to renew the certification as provided in this section may be reinstated by the board on:

**(1)** Payment of the renewal fee plus a penalty; and

**(2)** Submission of evidence that the person currently meets the requirements to serve as a medication assistive person.

**(e)** Any person providing services as a medication assistive person during the time his or her certification has lapsed shall be considered to be providing services illegally and shall be subject to the penalties provided for violations of this subchapter.

**History:**

Acts 2005, No. 1423, § 4.

## § 17-87-707. Disciplinary Actions

**(a)** The Arkansas State Board of Nursing shall have sole authority to deny, suspend, revoke, or limit any medication assistive person certificate issued by the board or applied for in accordance with the provisions of this subchapter or to otherwise discipline a certificate holder upon proof that the person:

**(1)** Has been found guilty of or pleads guilty or nolo contendere to:

**(A)** Fraud or deceit in procuring or attempting to procure a medication assistive person certificate;

**(B)** Providing services as a medication assistive person without a valid certificate; or

**(C)** Committing a crime of moral turpitude;

**(2)** Is unfit or incompetent by reason of negligence, habits, or other causes;

**(3)** Is habitually intemperate or is addicted to the use of habit-forming drugs;

**(4)** Is mentally incompetent;

**(5)** Is guilty of unprofessional conduct;

**(6)** Has had a license, certificate, or registration revoked or suspended;

**(7)** Has been placed on probation or under disciplinary order in any jurisdiction;

**(8)** Has voluntarily surrendered a license, certification, or registration and has not been reinstated in any jurisdiction; or

**(9)** Has willfully or repeatedly violated any of the provisions of this subchapter.

**(b)** The board shall refuse to issue or shall revoke the certificate of any person who would be disqualified from employment under the provisions of § 20-33-213.

**(c)** Proceedings under this section shall be conducted in accordance with the Arkansas Administrative Procedure Act, § 25-15-201 et seq.

**History:** Acts 2005, No. 1423, § 4, Act 2009, No. 762.

## § 17-87-708. Penalty

**(a) (1)** It shall be a misdemeanor for any person to:

**(A)** Sell or fraudulently obtain or furnish any medication assistive person's certificate, renewal, or record or aid or abet in any such sale or fraud;

**(B)** Serve as a medication assistive person under cover of any certificate or record illegally or fraudulently obtained or signed or issued unlawfully or under fraudulent representation;

**(C)** Serve as a medication assistive person unless certified by the Arkansas State Board of Nursing;

**(D)** Use in connection with his or her name any of the following titles, names, or initials if the user is not properly certified under this subchapter:

**(i)** Medication assistive person;

**(ii)** M.A.P.;

**(iii)** Medication aide;

**(iv)** Medication technician;

**(v)** Medication assistant;

**(vi)** Certified medication aide;

**(vii)** C.M.A.;

**(viii)** Medication assistant – Certified;

**(ix)** MA – C; or

**(x)** Any other name, title, or initials that would cause a reasonable person to believe the user is certified under this subchapter;

**(E)** Serve as a medication assistive person during the time his or her certification is suspended;

**(F)** Conduct an education program for the preparation of medication assistive persons unless the program has been approved by the board; or

**(G)** Otherwise violate any provisions of this subchapter.

**(2) (A)** A misdemeanor under subdivision (a)(1) of this section shall be punishable by a fine of not less than twenty-five dollars ($25.00) or more than five hundred dollars ($500).

**(B)** Each subsequent offense shall be punishable by a fine of not more than five hundred dollars ($500) or by imprisonment of not more than thirty (30) days, or by both a fine and imprisonment.

**(b) (1)** After providing notice and a hearing, the board may levy civil penalties in an amount not to exceed one thousand dollars ($1,000) against a person or entity for each violation of this subchapter or regulations promulgated under this subchapter.

**(2)** Each day of violation shall be a separate offense.

**(c)** Unless a penalty assessed under this section is paid within fifteen (15) calendar days following the date for an appeal from the order, the board may file suit in Pulaski County Circuit Court to obtain a judgment for the amount of penalty not paid.

**(d)** The penalties permitted in this section shall be in addition to other penalties that may be imposed by the board under this subchapter.

**History:**

Acts 2005, No. 1423, § 4; 2007, No. 206, § 2.

## § 17-87-709.  Injunction

(a) The Pulaski County Circuit Court is vested with jurisdiction and power to enjoin the unlawful provision of medication assistive person services in any county of the State of Arkansas in a proceeding initiated by the Arkansas State Board of Nursing, any member of the board, or any citizen in this state.

(b) (1) The issuance of an injunction shall not relieve a person from criminal prosecution for violation of the provisions of this subchapter.

(2) The remedy of injunction is to be in addition to liability for criminal prosecution.

**History:**

Acts 2005, No. 1423, § 4.

## § 17-87-710.  Medication Assistive Person Advisory Committee

(a) (1) The Medication Assistive Person Advisory Committee is created as an advisory committee to the Arkansas State Board of Nursing.

(2) The committee shall assist the board in implementing the provisions of this subchapter regarding medication assistive persons.

(b) The board shall appoint six (6) members to be approved by the Governor who have the following qualifications:

(1) Two (2) members shall be certified medication assistive persons;

(2) One (1) member shall be a licensed nursing home administrator who has worked in that capacity for at least five (5) years;

(3) One (1) member shall be a registered nurse who has been in a practice using certified nurse aides for at least five (5) years;

**(4)** One (1) member shall be a lay person representing the interest of consumers of health care services; and

**(5)** One (1) member shall be a nursing faculty member of an Arkansas nursing education program.

**(c)** Members shall serve three-year terms.

**(d)** The board may remove any committee member after notice and hearing for incapacity, incompetence, neglect of duty, or malfeasance in office.

**(e)** The members of the committee shall serve without compensation but may receive expense reimbursement in accordance with § 25-16-902.

**History:**

Acts 2005, No. 1423, § 4; 2007, No. 206, § 3.

## § 17-87-711.  Applicability of Subchapter

Nothing in this subchapter relieves a nurse from the responsibility of assessing each patient daily.

**History:**

Acts 2005, No. 1423, § 4.

# PART II

# ARKANSAS STATE BOARD OF NURSING RULES AND REGULATIONS

# CHAPTER ONE

## GENERAL PROVISIONS

### SECTION I
### PURPOSE AND AUTHORITY

**A. PURPOSE**

    **1. ARKANSAS NURSE PRACTICE ACT** – Requires that any person who practices or offers to practice professional nursing, advanced practice nursing, registered nurse practitioner nursing, practical nursing, or psychiatric technician nursing for compensation be licensed and submit evidence that he or she is qualified to so practice and shall be licensed as hereinafter provided.

    **2. ARKANSAS STATE BOARD OF NURSING** – Established by the Arkansas Nurse Practice Act for the implementation of the statute by carrying on the licensing or certification, disciplinary, and educational functions for professional, advanced practice, registered nurse practitioner, practical, and psychiatric technician nursing and medication assistants.

**B. LEGAL AUTHORITY** – The authority of the Board is contained in the ACA §17-87-101 et seq.

### SECTION II
### THE PRACTICE OF NURSING

**A. THE PRACTICE OF PROFESSIONAL NURSING**
The performance for compensation of any acts involving the observation, care, and counsel of the ill, injured, or infirm; the maintenance of health or prevention of illness of others; the supervision and teaching of other personnel; the delegation of certain nursing practices to other personnel as set forth in rules established by the board; or the administration of medications and treatments as prescribed by practitioners authorized to prescribe and treat according to state law where such acts require substantial specialized judgment and skill based on knowledge and application of the principles of biological, physical, and social sciences.

**B. THE PRACTICE OF ADVANCED PRACTICE NURSING**
The practice of advanced practice nursing means the delivery of health care services for compensation by professional nurses who have gained additional knowledge and skills through successful completion of an organized program of nursing education that certifies

nurses for advanced practice roles as advanced nurse practitioners, certified registered nurse anesthetists, certified nurse midwives, and clinical nurse specialists.

**1. ADVANCED NURSE PRACTITIONER** The practice of advanced nurse practitioner nursing means the performance for compensation of nursing skills by a registered nurse who, as demonstrated by national certification, has advanced knowledge and practice skill in the delivery of nursing services.

**2. CERTIFIED REGISTERED NURSE ANESTHETIST** The practice of certified registered nurse anesthesia means the performance for compensation of advanced nursing skills relevant to the administration of anesthetics under the supervision of, but not necessarily in the presence of, a licensed physician, licensed dentist, or other person lawfully entitled to order anesthesia.

**3. CERTIFIED NURSE MIDWIFE** The practice of nurse midwifery means the performance for compensation of nursing skills relevant to the management of women's health care, focusing on pregnancy, childbirth, the postpartum period, care of the newborn, family planning, and gynecological needs of women, within a health care system that provides for consultation, collaborative management, or referral as indicated by the health status of the client.

**4. CLINICAL NURSE SPECIALIST** The practice of clinical nurse specialist nursing means the performance for compensation of nursing skills by a registered nurse who, through study and supervised practice at the graduate level and as evidenced by national certification, has advanced knowledge and practice skills in a specialized area of nursing practice.

## C. THE PRACTICE OF REGISTERED NURSE PRACTITIONER NURSING
The delivery of health care services for compensation in collaboration with and under the direction of a licensed physician or under the direction of protocols developed with a licensed physician. Registered nurse practitioners shall be authorized to engage in activities as recognized by the nursing profession and as authorized by the Board. Nothing in this subdivision is to be deemed to limit a registered nurse practitioner from engaging in those activities which normally constitute the practice of nursing, or those which may be performed by persons without the necessity of the license to practice medicine.

## D. THE PRACTICE OF PRACTICAL NURSING
The performance for compensation of acts involving the care of the ill, injured, or infirm or the delegation of certain nursing practices to other personnel as set forth in rules established by the board; under the direction of a registered professional nurse, an advanced practice nurse, a licensed physician, or a licensed dentist, which acts do not require the substantial specialized skill, judgment, and knowledge required in professional nursing.

## E. THE PRACTICE OF PSYCHIATRIC TECHNICIAN NURSING

The performance for compensation of acts involving the care of the physically and mentally ill, retarded, injured, or infirm or the delegation of certain nursing practices to other personnel as set forth in rules established by the board, and the carrying out of medical orders under the direction of a registered professional nurse, an advanced practice nurse, a licensed physician or a licensed dentist, where such activities do not require the substantial specialized skill, judgment, and knowledge required in professional nursing.

## SECTION III
## IDENTIFICATION INSIGNIA

**A.** Any person who holds a license to practice nursing in this state shall use the legal title or the abbreviation as set forth in Arkansas Code Annotated Section 17-87-101, et seq. No other person shall assume any other name, title, or abbreviation or any words, letters, signs, or devices that would cause a reasonable person to believe the user is licensed to practice nursing.

**B.** Any person licensed to practice nursing shall wear an insignia to identify himself by his name and appropriate legal title or abbreviation during times when such person is providing health care to the public for compensation.

**C.** The insignia shall be prominently displayed and clearly legible such that the person receiving care may readily identify the type of nursing personnel providing such care.

## SECTION IV
## DEFINITION OF TERMS

**ACCREDITED** The status granted by an accrediting agency through a voluntary process.

**ACTIVITIES OF DAILY LIVING** Those self-care activities which must be accomplished each day in order for the client to care for his own needs and participate in society.

**ADVANCED PRACTICE NURSE CATEGORIES** Advanced nurse practitioner, certified registered nurse anesthetist, certified nurse midwife, and clinical nurse specialist.

**APPROVAL** Recognized by the Board as meeting the education standards for preparing graduates for registered or practical nurse licensure.

**APPROVAL TYPES:**

**PREREQUISITE** Status authorizing a program to proceed in establishing a program of nursing.

**INITIAL** Status awarded to a program that has met all initial requirements and authorizes the program to proceed to admission of students and completion of educational standards.

**FULL** Status awarded to a program that has met all educational standards.

**CONTINUED FULL** Status awarded to a program that continues to maintain the educational standards.

**CONDITIONAL** Status of a program that has not maintained the educational standards. Serves as a warning that if the standards are not followed withdrawal of approval may be initiated.

**BOARD** The Arkansas State Board of Nursing.

**BOARD REPRESENTATIVE** A person appointed, hired, or otherwise authorized by the Board to carry out its functions.

**CLINICAL FACILITY** A facility outside the framework of the program which provides educational experiences for the student.

**COLLABORATING PHYSICIAN** A physician, licensed under the Arkansas Medical Practices Act, § 17-93-201 et seq., who has a practice comparable in scope, specialty or expertise to that of the advanced practice nurse or registered nurse practitioner.

**COLLABORATIVE PRACTICE AGREEMENT** Document setting out how an advanced practice nurse and physician intend to cooperate in the delivery of client care.

**CONSULTING PHYSICIAN** A physician licensed by the Arkansas Medical Practices Act who has obstetric privileges in a hospital.

**CONTROLLED SUBSTANCE** Drug substance or immediate precursor in Schedules I-V.

**CREDENTIAL** A license, certificate, or other evidence of qualifications.

**DELEGATION** Entrusting the performance of a selected nursing task to an individual who is qualified, competent, and able to perform such tasks. The nurse retains the accountability for the total nursing care of the individual.

**DISTANT LEARNING SITE**  A location separate from the main campus where course offerings are delivered.

**DOCUMENTATION** Written proof or evidence to substantiate factual claims or statements satisfactory to the Board.

**DRUG SAMPLE**  A unit of a legend drug which is distributed to a practitioner by a manufacturer or a manufacturer's representative at no charge, is not intended to be sold, and is intended to promote the sale of the drug.

**EMERGENCY CARE**  Unanticipated care provided to a person who is unconscious, ill, or injured, when the circumstances require prompt decisions and actions, and when the necessity of immediate care is so apparent that any delay would seriously worsen the physical condition or endanger the life of the person.

**GRADUATE COMPETENCIES**  Educational outcomes expected of the nursing program's graduates.

**LEGEND DRUG**  A drug limited by Section 503(b)(1) of the Federal Food, Drug, and Cosmetic Act to being dispensed by or upon a practitioner's  prescription.

**MAY**  Indicates permission.

**MISSION**  Beliefs accepted by the parent institution for the framework of the school•fs programs and offerings.

**OBSERVATIONAL EXPERIENCE** One in which the nursing student provides no nursing care.

**PARENT INSTITUTION**  The official institution sponsoring the nursing program.

**PERSONAL CARE**  Assistance with activities of daily living not requiring a medical prescription.

**PHILOSOPHY**  Beliefs adopted by the nursing faculty for the framework of the program.

**PRECEPTOR**  A currently licensed nurse or physician, meeting the requirements of these rules, who serves as a facilitator of student learning in a practice setting.

**PRECEPTORSHIP**  Practice under the supervision of a qualified preceptor in the care of consumers of health services while a student in a Board approved program.

**PRESCRIPTIVE AUTHORITY** Authorization, given by the Board, for an advanced practice nurse who meets established requirements to prescribe. Prescriptive authority for controlled substances shall only extend to drugs listed in Schedules III through V.

**PROGRAM** The total educational curriculum in nursing, including theoretical and clinical components.

**Types of Programs are:**

**ASSOCIATE DEGREE PROGRAM** A professional nursing program leading to an associate degree with a major in nursing.

**BACCALAUREATE DEGREE PROGRAM** A professional nursing program leading to a baccalaureate degree with a major in nursing

**DIPLOMA PROGRAM** A professional nursing program leading to a diploma with a major in nursing.

**PRACTICAL NURSING PROGRAM** A nursing program leading to a certificate in practical nursing.

**PSYCHIATRIC TECHNICIAN NURSING PROGRAM** A nursing program leading to a certificate in psychiatric technician nursing.

**PROGRAM DIRECTOR** The person responsible for the specific educational unit in nursing, regardless of the official title in the institution.

**PROTOCOL** A written statement which delineates agreed-upon approaches in lient care and management.

**SATELLITE CAMPUS** A separate geographic location where a program is offered which has a separate student body and a separate faculty leader/coordinator and/or faculty.

**SHALL, WILL, MUST** Indicates a mandatory requirement.

**SHOULD** Indicates a recommendation.

**SURVEY** A visit to determine compliance with minimum requirements

**THERAPEUTIC DEVICE** An instrument or apparatus, requiring a prescription, that is intended for use in diagnosis or treatment, and in the prevention of disease or maintenance or restoration of health.

**TRANSMITTING** Relaying an order for a medication, treatment, or therapeutic device.

**UNDER THE DIRECTION OF A LICENSED PHYSICIAN** The performance of specific acts and procedures which have been authorized by a licensed physician and which may be performed outside the presence of the physician under conditions where a physician is readily available for consultation.

**UNENCUMBERED LICENSE** Free of disciplinary limitations or pending action.

## SECTION V
## GENERAL MATTERS

### A. OFFICE AND HOURS
The office of the Board is in Little Rock, Arkansas. The office shall be open during business hours each day; Saturday, Sunday, and holidays excepted.

### B. EXAMINATION, INQUIRY, OR INVESTIGATION
The Board may, through one or more of its members, or staff especially authorized, conduct at its office in Little Rock, Arkansas, or in any part of the state, any examination, inquiry or investigation, hearing, or other proceeding necessary to perform its duties and functions. The executive director shall have custody of the seal and official records and shall be responsible for the maintenance and custody of the files and records of the Board, including the credentials for all Arkansas licensed nurses, transcripts of testimony and exhibits, the minutes of all actions taken by the Board and all of its findings, determinations, reports, opinions, orders, rules, and approved forms.

### C. AUTHENTICATION
All notices and other actions of the Board shall be authenticated or signed by the president, secretary, or such other person as may be authorized by the Board.

### D. NOTICE
Upon order of the Board, the president, secretary, or executive director shall issue all notices of hearings and other process as may be directed by the Board.

### E. EXECUTIVE DIRECTOR
The executive director of the Board shall be a registered nurse and meet the qualifications required by the Board.

## F.  BOARD FUNDS AND FEES

1. The Board shall establish and collect fees for services relating to examination, licensing,endorsement, certification for prescriptive authority, temporary permits, license renewal, and other reasonable services as determined by the Board.

2. All funds received by the Board shall be deposited in the State Treasury to the credit of the Board.

3. Fees paid to the Board may be in the form of cash, cashier checks, or money orders. Personal checks for initial licensure are accepted from in-state residents only.

4. Fees paid to the Board are processing fees and are not refundable.

## G.  RECORDS

1. Record Maintenance
The executive director shall enter, in permanent form, credentials of all nurses, records of official transactions and proceedings, and keep such records in safekeeping.

2. Tapes
Meetings may be taped by a secretary as necessary for purposes of minute taking. Tapes may be erased after corresponding minutes have been approved.

3. Destruction
The executive director may destroy or dispose of records in the office in accord with applicable law.

4. Certified Copies
Upon written request and payment of a fee, the executive director shall provide to any nurse holding Arkansas licensure a certified copy of any of his or her records on file in the Board office.

5. Public Inspection
Records shall be open to public inspection except as may be specifically exempted by statute.

6. Request for Copies of Rules
Copies of rules of the Board will be furnished free of charge to any official of a government agency requesting them in the performance of his or her duties.

## H. EXAMINATION REVIEW

A registered nurse, practical nurse, or psychiatric technician nurse candidate who has failed the licensure examination may review his or her examination and/or challenge examination items according to the policies and procedures of the test development vendor.

## SECTION VI
## NURSING STUDENT LOAN PROGRAM

## A. ELIGIBILITY REQUIREMENTS

As funds are made available, any Arkansas resident who is enrolled in, or has been accepted for admission to, an approved school of nursing in this state or in a nationally accredited school outside the state, in a course of study leading to qualification as a registered nurse, licensed practical nurse, or nurse educator shall be eligible to make application to the Arkansas State Board of Nursing for a nursing educator loan or a nursing practice loan. The Board may, depending upon available funds, make a nursing educator loan or a nursing practice loan to an applicant when it determines that the applicant:

      1.      Warrants financial assistance to complete his or her nursing studies.

      2.      Has signed a written agreement to, upon graduation and licensure and for one year for each year a loan is granted:

      a. Teach in a nursing education program in the State of Arkansas if granted a nursing educator loan; or

      b. Engage in practice as a registered nurse or licensed practical nurse in the State of Arkansas if granted a nursing practice loan; and

      c. Repay each loan with interest at the maximum legal rate if the applicant fails to fulfill the requirements of the board.

## B. MAINTENANCE REQUIREMENTS

1. Subject to the availability of funds and the limits set out in these rules, each loan made to an applicant shall be renewable annually for the number of years required to complete studies leading to qualification as a registered nurse, license practical nurse, or nursing educator.

2. Any loan made to an applicant subsequent to an initial loan shall be made only upon application of the recipient and upon finding by the Arkansas State Board of Nursing that the applicant:

      a. Has successfully completed the nursing studies of the preceding academic year and remains in good standing as an enrolled student in the appropriate nursing program;

      b. Warrants financial assistance to complete his or her nursing studies;

c. Has signed a written agreement to, upon graduation and licensure and for one year for each year a loan is granted:

 i. Teach in a nursing education program in the State of Arkansas; or

 ii. Engage in practice as a registered nurse or licensed practical nurse in the State of Arkansas; and

 iii. Repay each loan with interest at the maximum legal rate if the applicant fails to fulfill the requirements of the board; and

d. Continues to be a lawful resident of the State of Arkansas.

3. The total of the loans made to any one (1) student shall not exceed twenty thousand dollars ($20,000).

## C. BORROWER'S LOSS OF GOOD STANDING

If the recipient of a loan ceases to be enrolled in good standing in a recognized nursing program before completing the education requirements to qualify as a registered nurse, licensed practical nurse, or nursing educator, the principal and interest of all loans made to the recipient shall become due and payable immediately or as provided in the loan agreement.

## D. LOAN REPAYMENT

1. A recipient of a loan shall repay each loan together with interest at the maximum rate allowed by Arkansas law if the recipient:

a. Ceases to be enrolled in good standing in a recognized nursing program before completing the education requirements to qualify as a registered nurse, licensed practical nurse, or nursing educator;

b. Does not, for the period specified in the agreement, teach in an Arkansas nursing education program if granted a nursing educator loan, or engage in practice as a registered nurse or licensed practical nurse in Arkansas if granted a nursing practice loan; or

c. Fails to comply with any other requirements of the agreement.

2. Interest shall accrue from the date each payment of funds was received by the recipient.

3. No interest shall accrue and no obligation to repay a loan exists during any period of time that the recipient of the loan serves on active duty in the United States armed forces.

4. If repayment of a loan is required, upon the death of the recipient of the loan all unpaid principal and interest is due and payable.

5. The failure to repay a loan as specified may be considered unprofessional conduct for disciplinary purposes.

# CHAPTER TWO

## LICENSURE: RN, LPN, AND LPTN

### SECTION I
### QUALIFICATIONS

**A.** Good moral character.

**B.** Completion of an approved high school course of study or the equivalent as determined by the appropriate educational agency.

**C.** Completion of the required approved nursing education program. (LPN and LPTN requirements may be waived if applicant is determined to be otherwise qualified.)

**D.** The Arkansas State Board of Nursing (ASBN) may refuse to admit to the examination any candidate and refuse to issue a license, certificate, or registration to any applicant if the license, practice privilege, certificate, or registration of such person has been revoked or suspended or placed on probation and not reinstated by the jurisdiction which took such action.

**E.** Effective January 1, 2000, no person shall be eligible to receive or hold a license issued by the Board if that person has pleaded guilty or nolo contendere to, or been found guilty by any court in the State of Arkansas, or of any similar offense by a court in another state, or of any similar offense by a federal court of any offense listed in ACA §17-87-312.

### SECTION II
### EXAMINATION

#### A. ELIGIBILITY
The applicant shall meet the licensure requirements of the Board.

#### B. APPLICATION

    1. Applications for examination shall be completed and filed with the Board prior to the examination.

    2. Examination applications shall not be acceptable if the director or chairman of an educational program has certified the applicant prior to date of completion.

    3. Applicants for licensure by examination shall not be deemed eligible to take the licensure examination until such time that the results of the state and federal criminal background checks have been received.

## C. FEE

1. The examination fee shall accompany the application.
2. The examination fee (first time or retake) is not refundable.
3. The fees for the state and federal criminal background checks are the responsibility of the applicant and shall be submitted to the Arkansas State Board of Nursing with the application for same.
4. The fees are determined by the Arkansas State Police and the FBI and are not refundable.

## D. PASSING SCORE

The passing score on the licensure examination shall be determined by the Board.

## E. FAILING SCORE AND ELIGIBILITY TO RETAKE THE EXAMINATION

1. Any applicant whose score falls below the passing score shall fail the examination.
2. Persons failing the examination will be responsible for preparing to retake the examination.
3. The frequency and number of retests by unsuccessful candidates shall be determined by the Board.
4. Applicants retaking the examination shall have state and federal criminal background checks within the past twelve months on file with the Board.

## F. RESULTS

1. Examination results shall not be released until the applicant's transcript is received from the school.
2. Examination results shall be mailed to all applicants and to their respective schools.

## G. INTERNATIONALLY EDUCATED NURSES

1. The applicant must present evidence of:
    a. Graduation from an approved or accredited school of nursing. The Board may waive this requirement for LPN and LPTN applicants provided they are otherwise qualified.
    b. Licensure or proof of eligibility for licensure in the country of graduation.
    c. Theory and practice in medical, surgical, pediatric, obstetric, and psychiatric nursing which is substantially similar in length and content to that in equivalent Arkansas Board approved nursing programs at the time of application as verified by a credentials review agency.
    d. State and federal criminal background checks within the past twelve months on file with the Board.

e. Credentials review that includes verification of the candidate's education, training, experience, and licensure with respect to the statutory and regulatory requirements for the nursing profession, as well as oral and written competence in English.

2. Transcripts and certificates which are not in English must be accompanied by a certified translation.

3. Applicants shall be required to take such licensure examinations as required of Arkansas Board approved nursing programs.

## H. EQUIVALENCIES

1. LPTN to LPN: Candidates holding LPTN licensure who completed Arkansas Board approved LPTN programs after March 18, 1980, may be admitted to the LPN licensure examination provided they are otherwise qualified.

2. RN examination failures: Graduates of Board approved RN programs, upon submission of an official transcript directly from the school, and a copy of their RN examination failure results, may be admitted to the PN licensure examination provided they are otherwise qualified.

3. Portion of RN Program: Candidates who have completed equivalent courses in a state approved program of nursing may be admitted to the PN licensure examination provided they are otherwise qualified. Evidence must be provided verifying successful completion of classroom instruction and clinical practice substantially similar to the minimum requirements for practical nursing programs.

## SECTION III
### INTERSTATE NURSE LICENSURE COMPACT

## A. DEFINITIONS OF TERMS IN THE COMPACT
For the purpose of the Compact:

1. "Board" means party state's regulatory body responsible for issuing nurse licenses.

2. "Information system" means the coordinated licensure information system.

3. "Primary state of residence" means the state of a person's declared fixed permanent and principal home for legal purposes; domicile.

4. "Public" means any individual or entity other than designated staff or representatives of party state Boards or the National Council of State Boards of Nursing, Inc.

5. "Alternative program" means a voluntary, non-disciplinary monitoring program approved by a nurse licensing board.

6. "Coordinated Licensure Information System" means an integrated process for collecting, storing, and sharing information on nurse licensure and enforcement activities related to nurse licensure laws, which is administered by a non-profit organization composed

of state nurse licensing boards.

7. "Home state" means the party state which is the nurse's primary state of residence.

8. "Multi-state licensure privilege" means current, official authority from a remote state permitting the practice of nursing as either a registered nurse or a licensed practical/vocational nurse in such party state.

9. "Nurse" means a registered nurse or licensed practical nurse, as those terms are defined by each party's state practice laws.

10. "Party state" means any state that has adopted this Compact.

11. "Remote state" means a party state, other than the home state,

(a) where the patient is located at the time nursing care is provided, or,

(b) in the case of the practice of nursing not involving a patient, in such party state where the recipient of nursing practice is located.

12. "Current significant investigative information" means:

(a) investigative information that a licensing board, after a preliminary inquiry that includes notification and an opportunity for the nurse to respond if required by state law, has reason to believe is not groundless and, if proved true, would indicate more than a minor infraction; or

(b) investigative information that indicates that the nurse represents an immediate threat to public health and safety regardless of whether the nurse has been notified and had an opportunity to respond.

13. Licensed Practical Nurse or Licensed Vocational Nurse means a person who has been licensed as an LPN or LVN by a party state licensing board.

Other terms used in these rules are to be defined as in the Interstate Compact.

## B. ISSUANCE OF A LICENSE BY A COMPACT PARTY STATE

For the purpose of this Compact:

1. No applicant for initial licensure will be issued a compact license granting a multi-state privilege to practice unless the applicant first obtains a passing score on the applicable NCLEX examination or any other predecessor examination used for licensure.

2. A nurse applying for a license in a home party state shall produce evidence of the nurses' primary state of residence. Such evidence shall include a declaration signed by the licensee. Further evidence that may be requested may include but is not limited to:

a. Driver's license with a home address;

b. Voter registration card displaying a home address;

c. Federal income tax return declaring the primary state of residence;

d. Military form No. 2058-state of legal residence certificate; or

e. W2 from US Government or any bureau, division or agency thereof indicating the declared state of residence.

3. A nurse on a visa from another country applying for licensure in a party state may declare either the country of origin or the party state as the primary state of residence. If the foreign country is declared the primary state of residence, a single state license will be issued

by the party state.

4. A license issued by a party state is valid for practice in all other party states unless clearly designated as valid only in the state which issued the license.

5. When a party state issues a license authorizing practice only in that state and not authorizing practice in other party states (i.e. single state license), the license shall be clearly marked with words indicating that it is valid only in the state of issuance.

6. A nurse changing primary state of residence, from one party state to another party state, may continue to practice under the former home state license and multistate licensure privilege during the processing of the nurse's licensure application in the new home state for a period not to exceed thirty (30) days.

7. The licensure application in the new home state of a nurse under pending investigation by the former home state shall be held in abeyance and the thirty (30) day period in section B.6. shall be stayed until resolution of the pending investigation.

8. The former home state license shall no longer be valid upon the issuance of a new home state license.

9. If a decision is made by the new home state denying licensure, the new home state shall notify the former home state within ten (10) business days and the former home state may take action in accordance with that state's laws and rules.

10. Party states shall recognize and honor either the LPN or LVN title used for Licensed Practical Nurses and Licensed Vocational Nurses, respectively.

## C. LIMITATIONS ON MULTISTATE LICENSURE PRIVILEGE-DISCIPLINE

1. Home state Boards shall include in all licensure disciplinary orders and/or agreements that limit practice and/or require monitoring the requirement that the licensee subject to said order and/or agreement will agree to limit the licensee's practice to the home state during the pendency of the disciplinary order and/or agreement. This requirement may, in the alternative, allow the nurse to practice in other party states with prior written authorization from both the home state and such other party state Boards.

2. An individual who had a license which was surrendered, revoked, suspended, or an application denied for cause in a prior state of primary residence, may be issued a single state license in a new primary state of residence until such time as the individual would be eligible for an unrestricted license by the prior state(s) adverse action. Once eligible for licensure in the prior state(s), a multistate license may be issued.

## D. INFORMATION SYSTEM

1. Levels of access
   a. The public shall have access to nurse licensure information limited to:
      (1) The nurse's name;
      (2) Jurisdiction(s) of licensure;
      (3) License expiration date(s);

71

(4) Licensure classification(s) and status(es);

(5) Public emergency and final disciplinary actions, as defined by contributing state authority; and

(6) The status of multistate licensure privileges.

b. Non-party state Boards shall have access to all Information System data except current significant investigative information and other information as limited by contributing party state authority.

c. Party state Boards shall have access to all Information System data contributed by the party states and other information as limited by contributing non-party state authority.

2. The licensee may request in writing to the home state Board to review the data relating to the licensee in the Information System. In the event a licensee asserts that any data relating to him or her is inaccurate, the burden of proof shall be upon the licensee to provide evidence that substantiates such claim. The Board shall verify and within ten (10) business days correct inaccurate data to the Information System.

3. The Board shall report to the Information System within ten (10) business days:

a. Disciplinary action, agreement, or order requiring participation in alternative programs or which limit practice or require monitoring (except agreements and orders relating to participation in alternative programs required to remain nonpublic by contributing state authority);

b. Dismissal of complaint, and

c. Changes in status of disciplinary action, or licensure encumbrance.

4. Current significant investigative information shall be deleted from the Information System within ten (10) business days upon report of disciplinary action, agreement, or order requiring participation in alternative programs or agreements which limit practice or require monitoring or dismissal of a complaint.

5. Changes to licensure information in the Information System shall be completed within ten (10) business days upon notification by a Board.

# SECTION IV
# ENDORSEMENT

## A. ELIGIBILITY

1. An applicant for licensure by endorsement must meet the requirements of the Board at the time of graduation.

2. An applicant licensed in another state after January 1950 must have taken a state board licensing examination and achieved a passing score.

3. LPTN applicants will be accepted from California and Kansas only.

4. Internationally educated nurses practicing in other states may appeal to the Board for licensure if not otherwise qualified.

## B. EQUIVALENCIES

1. RN examination failures: Graduates of Board approved RN programs, holding LPN licensure by examination in other jurisdictions, may be endorsed provided they are otherwise qualified.

2. Canadian Registered Nurses licensed by NLN State Board Test Pool Examination in the following provinces during the years indicated: Alberta, 1952-1970; British Columbia, 1949-1970; Manitoba, 1955-1970; Newfoundland, 1961-1970; Nova Scotia, 1955-1970; Prince Edward Island, 1956-1970; Quebec (English language), 1959-1970; and Saskatchewan, 1956-1970. These applicants may be endorsed provided they are otherwise qualified.

3. Portion of RN Program: Candidates who have completed equivalent courses in a state approved program of nursing may be endorsed provided they are otherwise qualified. Evidence must be provided verifying successful completion of classroom instruction and clinical practice substantially similar to the minimum requirements for practical nursing programs.

## C. APPLICATION

1. Applications must be completed and filed with the Board.

2. Endorsement certification will be accepted from the state of original licensure only.

3. Applicants for licensure by endorsement shall not be issued a permanent license to practice until such time that the results of the state and federal criminal background checks have been received.

## D. FEE

1. The endorsement fee must accompany the application.

2. The fees for state and federal criminal background checks are the responsibility

of the applicant and shall be submitted to the Arkansas State Board of Nursing with the application for same.

    3. The fees are not refundable.

# SECTION V
## CRIMINAL BACKGROUND CHECK

**A.** No application for issuance of an initial license will be considered without state and federal criminal background checks by the Arkansas State Police and the Federal Bureau of Investigation.

**B.** Each applicant shall sign a release of information on the criminal background check application and licensure applications and shall be solely responsible for the payment of any fees associated with the state and federal criminal background checks.

**C.** Upon completion of the state and federal criminal background checks, the Identification Bureau of the Arkansas State Police shall forward all information obtained concerning the applicant in the commission of any offense listed in ACA § 17-87-312.

**D.** The state and federal criminal background checks conducted by the Arkansas State Police and the Federal Bureau of Investigation shall have been completed no earlier than twelve (12) months prior to the application for an initial license issued by the ASBN and at any other time thereafter that the Board deems necessary.

**E.** The ASBN shall not issue a permanent license until the state and federal criminal background checks conducted by the Arkansas State Police and the Federal Bureau of Investigation have been completed.

**F.** A request to seek waiver of the denial of licensure pursuant to the provisions of ACA § 17-87-312 may be made to the ASBN by:
    1. The affected applicant for licensure; or
    2. The person holding a license subject to revocation.

**G.** The request for a waiver shall be made in writing to the Executive Director or the designee within thirty (30) calendar days after notification of denial of a license. The request for waiver shall include, but not be limited to the following:
    1. Certified copy of court records indicating grounds for conviction; and
    2. Any other pertinent documentation to indicate surrounding circumstances.

**H.** If an individual notifies ASBN in writing that he or she desires a hearing regarding their request for a waiver, the ASBN will schedule the individual for a hearing pursuant to the

Arkansas Administrative Procedures Act.

**I.** In compliance with ACA § 17-87-312, whenever a criminal background check is performed on a person under the provisions of the criminal background check requirement contained in the Arkansas Code for licensure, the person may be disqualified for licensure if it is determined that the person committed a violation of any sexual offense formerly proscribed under ACA §§ 5-14-101 through 5-14-127 that is substantially equivalent to any sexual offense presently listed in Arkansas Code §§ 5-14-101 through 5-14-127 and is an offense screened for in a criminal background check.

## SECTION VI
## TEMPORARY PERMITS

### A. ENDORSEMENT AND EXAM APPLICANTS

1. ASBN shall be authorized to issue a temporary permit for a period not exceeding six months. This temporary permit shall be issued only to those applicants who meet all other qualifications for licensure by the ASBN.

2. The temporary permit shall immediately become invalid upon receipt of information obtained from the state or federal criminal background check indicating any offense listed in ACA §17-87-312 or upon notification to the applicant or ASBN of results on the first licensure examination he or she is eligible to take after the permit is issued.

3. Falsification of the applicant's criminal record history shall be grounds for disciplinary action by the Board.

### B. FEES AND APPLICATIONS

1. The temporary permit fee shall be submitted with the application.
2. The fee is not refundable.

## SECTION VII
## CONTINUING EDUCATION

Each person holding an active license or applying for reinstatement of a license under the provisions of the Nurse Practice Act shall be required to complete certain continuing education requirements prior to licensure renewal or reinstatement.

## A. DECLARATION OF COMPLIANCE

Each nurse shall declare his or her compliance with the requirements for continuing education at the time of license renewal or reinstatement. The declaration shall be made on the form supplied by the Board.

## B. AUDITS OF LICENSEES

1. The Board shall perform random audits of licensees for compliance with the continuing education requirement.

2. If audited, the licensee shall prove participation in the required continuing education during the 24-months immediately preceding the renewal date by presenting photocopies of original certificates of completion to the Board.

3. The licensee shall provide evidence of continuing education requirements within thirty (30) calendar days from the mailing date of the audit notification letter sent from the Board to the last known address of the licensee.

## C. CONTINUING EDUCATION REQUIREMENT STANDARDS

1. Standards for Renewal of Active Licensure Status. Licensees who hold an active nursing license shall document completion of one of the following during each renewal period:

    a. Fifteen (15) practice focused contact hours from a nationally recognized or state continuing education approval body recognized by the ASBN; or

    b. Certification or re-certification during the renewal period by a national certifying body recognized by the ASBN; or

    c. An academic course in nursing or related field; and

    d. Provide other evidence as requested by the Board.

    e. Effective January 1, 2010, APNs with prescriptive authority shall complete five (5) contact hours of pharmacotherapeutics continuing education in the APN's area of certification each biennium prior to license renewal.

2. Standards for Nurses on Inactive Status. Nurses who have their license placed on inactive status have no requirements for continuing education.

3. Standards for Reinstatement of Active Licensure Status

    a. Nurses reinstating a nursing license to active status after five years or less shall document completion of the following within the past two (2) years:

        i) Twenty (20) practice focused contact hours within the past two years from a nationally recognized or state continuing education approval body recognized by the ASBN, or

        ii) Certification or re-certification by a national certifying body recognized by the ASBN; or

        iii) An academic course in nursing or related field; and/or

iv) Provide other evidence as requested by the Board.

b. Nurses reinstating a nursing license to active status after greater than five years shall document completion of the following within the past two (2) years:

i) Twenty (20) practice focused contact hours within the past two years from a nationally recognized or state continuing education approval body recognized by the Arkansas State Board of Nursing, or

ii) Certification or re-certification by a national certifying body recognized by the ASBN; or

iii) An academic course in nursing or related field; and

iv) A refresher course approved by the ASBN; or

v) An employer competency orientation program, and

vi) Provide other evidence as requested by the Board.

4. Standards for Reinstatement of Prescriptive Authority Effective January 1, 2010, APNs whose prescriptive authority is inactive shall complete five (5) contact hours of pharmacotherapeutics continuing education in the APN's area of certification for each 12 months of non-prescribing activity in addition to the five (5) contact hours required for APN license renewal prior to reactivation of prescriptive authority.

5. The Board may issue a temporary permit to a nurse during the time enrolled in a Board approved nursing refresher course or an employer competency orientation program upon submission of an application, fees, and verification of enrollment in such program.

6. Continuing education hours beyond the required contact hours shall not be "carried over" to the next renewal period.

## D. RESPONSIBILITIES OF THE INDIVIDUAL LICENSEE

1. It shall be the responsibility of each licensee to select and participate in those continuing activities that will meet the criteria for acceptable continuing education as specified in ACA § 17-87-207 and these rules.

2. It shall be the licensee's responsibility to maintain records of continuing education as well as documented proof such as original certificates of attendance, contact hour certificates, academic transcripts or grade slips and to submit copies of this evidence when requested by the Board.

3. Records shall be maintained by the licensee for a minimum of two consecutive renewal periods or four years.

## E. RECOGNITION OF PROVIDERS

1. The Board shall identify organizations, agencies, and groups that shall be recognized as valid approval bodies/providers of nursing continuing education. The recognition may include providers approved by national organizations and state agencies with comparable standards.

2. The Board shall work with professional organizations, approved nursing schools,

and other providers of continuing educational programs to ensure that continuing education activities are available to nurses in Arkansas.

## F.  ACTIVITIES ACCEPTABLE FOR CONTINUING EDUCATION

1. Activities presented by recognized providers which may be acceptable include: national/regional educational conferences, classroom instruction, individualized instruction (home study/programmed instruction), academic courses, and institutional based instruction; and

2. The content shall be relevant to nursing practice and provide for professional growth of the licensee.

3. If participation is in an academic course or other program in which grades are given, a grade equivalent to "C" or better shall be required, or "pass" on a pass/fail grading system. An academic course may also be taken as "audit", provided that class attendance is verified by the instructor.

## G.  ACTIVITIES WHICH ARE NOT ACCEPTABLE AS CONTINUING EDUCATION

1. In-service programs. Activities intended to assist the nurse to acquire, maintain, and/or increase the competence in fulfilling the assigned responsibilities specific to the expectations of the employer.

2. Refresher courses. Programs designed to update basic general knowledge and clinical practice, which consist of a didactic and clinical component to ensure entry-level competencies into nursing practice.

3. Orientation programs. A program by which new staff are introduced to the philosophy, goals, policies, procedures, role expectations, physical facilities, and special services in a specific work setting. Orientation is provided at the time of employment and at other times when changes in roles and responsibilities occur in a specific work setting.

4.  Courses designed for lay people.

## H.  INDIVIDUAL REVIEW OF A CONTINUING EDUCATION ACTIVITY PROVIDED BY A NONRECOGNIZED AGENCY/ORGANIZATION

1. A licensee may request an individual review by:
    a. Submitting an "Application for Individual Review"; and
    b. Paying a fee.
2. Approval of a non-recognized continuing educational activity shall be limited to the specific event under consideration.

## I. FAILURE TO COMPLY

1. Any licensee who fails to complete continuing education or who falsely certifies completion of continuing education shall be subject to disciplinary action, non-renewal of the nurse's license, or both, pursuant to ACA §17-87-207 and A.C.A §17-87-309 (a)(1) and (a)(6).

2. If the Board determines that a licensee has failed to comply with continuing education requirements, the licensee will:

a. Be allowed to meet continuing education requirements within ninety (90) days of notification of non-compliance.

b. Be assessed a late fee for each contact hour that requirements are not met after the ninety (90) day grace period and be issued a Letter of Reprimand. Failure to pay the fee may result in further disciplinary action.

## SECTION VIII
## RENEWALS

**A.** Each person licensed under the provisions of the Nurse Practice Act shall renew biennially.

1. Sixty (60) days prior to the expiration date, the Board shall mail a renewal notice to the last known address of each nurse to whom a license was issued or renewed during the current period.

2. The application shall be completed before the license renewal is processed.

3. The fee for renewal shall accompany the application.

4. The fee is not refundable.

5. Pursuant to Act 996 of 2003 and upon written request and submission of appropriate documentation, members of the Armed Forces of the United States who are Arkansas residents and are ordered to active duty to a duty station located outside of this state shall be allowed an extension without penalty or assessment of a late fee for renewing the service members nursing license. The extension shall be effective for the period that the service member is serving on active duty at a duty station located outside of this state and for a period not to exceed six months after the service member returns to the state.

## B. LAPSED LICENSE

1. The license is lapsed if not renewed or placed in inactive status by the expiration date.

2. Failure to receive the renewal notice at the last address of record in the Board office shall not relieve the licensee of the responsibility for renewing the license by the expiration date.

3. Any licensee whose license has lapsed shall file a renewal application and pay the current renewal fee and the late fee.

4. Any person practicing nursing during the time his or her license has lapsed shall be considered an illegal practitioner and shall be subject to the penalties provided for violation of the Nurse Practice Act.

## C. INACTIVE STATUS

1. Any licensee in good standing, who desires to retire temporarily from the practice of nursing in this state, shall submit a request in writing and the current license shall be placed on inactive status.

2. While inactive, the licensee shall not practice nursing nor be subject to the payment of renewal fees.

3. When the licensee desires to resume practice, he or she shall request a renewal application, which shall be completed and submitted with a reinstatement fee and the renewal fee and must meet those requirements outlined in Section VII.

4. When disciplinary proceedings have been initiated against an inactive licensee, the license shall not be reinstated until the proceedings have been completed.

## D. RETIRED NURSE

1. Any licensee in good standing, who desires to retire for any length of time from the practice of nursing in this state, shall submit a request in writing, surrender the current license, and pay the required fee and the current license shall be placed on inactive status and a retired license issued.

2. A retired license shall be renewed biennially following submission of a renewal application and fee.

3. Fees are non-refundable.

4. While retired, the licensee shall not practice nursing, however:

    a. A registered nurse with a retired license may use the title "Registered Nurse", or the abbreviation "RN"; and

    b. A practical nurse with a retired license may use the title "Licensed Practice Nurse", or the abbreviation "LPN"; and

    c. A psychiatric technician nurse with a retired license may use the title "Licensed Psychiatric Technician Nurse", or the abbreviation "LPTN".

5. When the licensee desires to resume practice, he or she shall request a renewal application, which shall be completed and submitted with a reinstatement fee and the active renewal fee. The licensee must also meet those requirements outlined in Section VII.

6. If the retired license is allowed to lapse, the licensee shall not hold himself or herself out as an RN, LPN, or LPTN and shall pay a reinstatement fee in addition to the fee required for renewal of the retired license.

7. When disciplinary proceedings have been initiated against a retired licensee, the

license shall not be reinstated until the proceedings have been completed.

**E.** The licensee may be required to submit to a state and federal criminal background check if the Board deems it necessary.

## SECTION IX
## DUPLICATE LICENSE

**A.** A duplicate license or certificate shall be issued when the licensee submits a statement to the Board that the document is lost, stolen, or destroyed, and pays the required fee.

**B.** The license will be marked "duplicate".

## SECTION X
## CERTIFICATION/VERIFICATION TO ANOTHER JURISDICTION

Upon payment of a certification/verification fee, a nurse seeking licensure in another state may have a certified statement of Arkansas licensure issued to the Board of Nursing in that state.

## SECTION XI
## NAME OR ADDRESS CHANGE

**A.** A licensee, whose name is legally changed, shall be issued a replacement license following submission of the current license, along with a notarized statement, copy of marriage license, or court action, and the required fee.

**B.** A licensee, whose address changes from the address appearing on the current license, shall immediately notify the Board in writing of the change.

# CHAPTER THREE
# REGISTERED NURSE PRACTITIONER

## SECTION I
## SCOPE OF PRACTICE

### A. REGISTERED NURSE PRACTITIONER

A registered nurse practitioner is a licensed professional nurse prepared in the manner stated herein who provides direct care to individuals, families, and other groups in a variety of settings, including homes, hospitals, offices, industry, schools, and other institutions and health care settings. The service provided by the nurse practitioner is directed toward the delivery of primary, secondary, and tertiary care which focuses on the achievement and maintenance of optimal functions in the population. The nurse practitioner engages in independent decision making about the nursing care needs of clients and collaborates with health professionals and others in making decisions about other health care needs. The practitioner plans and institutes health care programs as a member of the health care team. The nurse practitioner is directly accountable and responsible to the recipient for the quality of care rendered. Rules which apply to registered nurses are hereby incorporated by reference.

### B. ACTS PROPER TO BE PERFORMED BY A REGISTERED NURSE PRACTITIONER

1. The Arkansas State Board of Nursing authorizes the registered nurse practitioner, in collaboration with and under the direction of a licensed physician, to perform particular acts at the advanced and specialized levels as recognized by the nursing profession and which are in conformity with the Nurse Practice Act.

a. Secures, records, and evaluates the health, psychosocial, and developmental history of patients;

b. Performs physical examinations using techniques of observation, inspection, auscultation, palpation and percussion, and uses appropriate diagnostic tests;

c. Discriminates between normal and abnormal findings on the history and physical examination and refers the individuals who need further evaluation or supervision;

d. Documents the processes of nursing care delivery;

e. Contributes to the comprehensive care of the ill in collaboration with the health care team;

f. Coordinates health care plans to enhance the quality of health care and diminish both fragmentation and duplication of service;

g. Contributes to the health education of individuals and groups and applies methods designed to increase each person's motivation to assume responsibility for his own health care;

h. Facilitates entry into and through the health care system by appropriate route;

i. Counsels with families and/or individuals regarding family planning, pregnancy, child care, emotional stresses, long term illness, and general health problems;

j. Performs periodic health evaluations and plans for health maintenance of clients; and

k. Conducts community clinics for case finding and screening for health problems.

2. The Arkansas State Board of Nursing authorizes the registered nurse practitioner, in collaboration with and under the direction of a licensed physician, to perform particular acts recognized by the nursing profession and which are in conformity with the Nurse Practice Act.

a. Assumes responsibility for ongoing health maintenance and clinical management of stable chronically ill patients;

b. Provides initial care of emergencies and initiates arrangements for continuing definitive care;

c. Identifies, manages, and initiates treatment for common medical problems by "Protocols" as described in Section I.C.; and

d. Evaluates progress and manages prenatal and postpartum care.

## C. PROTOCOLS

1. Any nurse practicing as a registered nurse practitioner shall practice in accordance with protocols developed in collaboration with and signed by a licensed physician.

2. Protocols shall address:

a. Established procedures for the management of common medical problems in the practice setting;

b. The degree to which collaboration, independent action, and supervision are required; and

c. Acts including, but not limited to, assessment, diagnosis, treatment, and evaluation.

3. Protocols shall not include controlled substances.

4. Documentation.

a. Orders transmitted from protocols shall be documented on the client's medical record;

b. Orders transmitted from protocols to inpatient medical records shall contain:

(1) Name of medication, therapeutic device, or treatment;

(2) Strength;

(3) Dose;

(4) Length of time or amount prescribed;

(5) Directions for use;

(6) RNP Signature; and

(7) Physician's name, printed, followed by notation "protocol."

5. Any deviation from written protocols shall require:

a. A specific written or verbal order from the collaborating physician before the order is transmitted or implemented; and

b. Documentation in the medical record as specified in §b (1)-(6) above, and notation that order was by consultation, to be signed by the RNP.

6. Review of Protocols

a. The RNP shall document annual joint review with the licensed physician, and revise when necessary.

b. The RNP shall, upon request, provide the Board with current protocols.

7. Nothing in this regulation shall be construed to prohibit any registered nurse practitioner from transmitting a prescription order orally or telephonically, or from administering a legend drug pursuant to a lawful direction of a licensed physician, dentist, or advanced practice nurse who holds a certificate of prescriptive authority.

## D. SERVICES AND RESPONSIBILITIES

The RNP shall, upon request of the Board, provide documentation outlining the extent of services, responsibilities, and required supervision of nurse practitioners, and the accompanying responsibilities of collaborating physicians.

## E. DELEGATED ACTS

The registered nurse practitioner shall demonstrate competence in any act or procedure delegated by the collaborating physician.

## SECTION II
## LICENSURE

**A.** Initial licensing of registered nurse practitioners terminated on November 30, 2000.

## B. RENEWAL

1. The date for renewal of licensure to practice as a registered nurse practitioner shall coincide with the renewal of the applicant's registered nurse license.

2. An application for renewal of a registered nurse practitioner license shall submit to the Board:

a. A completed application form; and

b. Payment of the nonrefundable renewal fee.

## C.  LAPSED LICENSE

1.  The license is lapsed if not renewed or placed in an inactive status by the expiration date.

2.  Failure to receive the renewal notice shall not relieve the licensee of the responsibility for renewing the license by the expiration date.

3.  Any licensee whose license has lapsed shall submit to the Board:
    a. A completed Board renewal application form; and
    b. The renewal fee and the reinstatement fee.

4.  Fees are nonrefundable.

5.  Any person practicing as a registered nurse practitioner during the time his or her license has lapsed shall be considered an illegal practitioner and shall be subjected to the penalties provided for violation of the Nurse Practice Act.

## D.  INACTIVE STATUS

1. Any licensee in good standing who desires his or her registered nurse practitioner license to be placed on inactive status may submit a request in writing to the Board.

2. The current license shall be placed on inactive status.

3. While the license is inactive, the licensee shall not engage in registered nurse practitioner nursing nor be subject to the payment of renewal fees.

4. If the nurse desires to resume practice, he or she shall submit a written request for a renewal application, which shall be completed and submitted with a renewal fee and the reinstatement fee.

5. Fees are nonrefundable.

6. If disciplinary proceedings on an inactive licensee have been initiated, the license shall not be reinstated until the proceedings have been completed.

## SECTION III
## DUPLICATE LICENSE

**A.** The licensee shall immediately report a lost, stolen, or destroyed license to the Board.

**B.** A duplicate license shall be issued when the licensee submits a notarized statement to the Board that the document is lost, stolen, or destroyed, and pays the required fee.

**C.** The license will be marked "duplicate".

# SECTION IV
## NAME OR ADDRESS CHANGE

**A.** A licensee whose name is legally changed shall be issued a replacement license following submission of the current license, along with an affidavit, copy of marriage license or court action, and the required fee.

**B.** A licensee, whose address changes from the address appearing on the current license, shall immediatelynotify the Board in writing of the change.

# CHAPTER FOUR
## ADVANCED PRACTICE NURSING

# SECTION I
## SCOPE OF PRACTICE

The advanced practice nurse shall practice in a manner consistent with the definition of the practice of advanced practice nursing set forth in Arkansas Code Annotated § 17-87-102 (4).(A) (B) (C)(D), and in accordance with the scope of practice defined by the appropriate national certifying body and the standards set forth in these rules. The advanced practice nurse (APN) may provide health care for which the APN is educationally prepared and for which competence has been attained and maintained.

# SECTION II
## QUALIFICATIONS FOR LICENSURE

Advanced practice nurse (APN) licensure shall be designated in one of the four roles below and at least one population focus – Family/Individual Across the Lifespan, Adult-Gerontology, Neonatal, Pediatrics, Women's Health/Gender-related, or Psychiatric/Mental Health (effective 2015). A current, unencumbered registered nurse license to practice in Arkansas is required for all categories of advanced practice licensure. Effective January 1, 2003, all applicants for advanced practice licensure by examination shall have completed a graduate level advanced practice nursing education program. Applicants for advanced practice licensure by endorsement shall have met the educational and certification requirements set forth in Arkansas State Board of Nursing Rules at the time of their initial licensure as an advanced practice nurse in another jurisdiction.

APN roles and their respective qualifications are:

## A. ADVANCED NURSE PRACTITIONER (ANP)

1. Successful completion of an organized program of nursing education that prepares nurses for the advanced practice role of advanced nurse practitioner; and

2. Current certification as a nurse practitioner by a nationally recognized certifying body which meets the requirements of Section VII of this Chapter.

## B. CERTIFIED REGISTERED NURSE ANESTHETIST (CRNA)

1. Successful completion, beyond generic nursing preparation, of a formal educational program that meets the standards of the Council on Accreditation of Nurse Anesthesia Educational Programs or another nationally recognized accrediting body that has as its objective preparation of nurses to perform as nurse anesthetists; and

2. Current certification from the Council on Certification of Nurse Anesthetists, Council on Recertification of Nurse Anesthetists, or another nationally recognized certifying body which meets the requirements of Section VII of this Chapter.

## C. CERTIFIED NURSE MIDWIFE (CNM)

1. Successful completion of an organized program of nursing education program that prepares nurses for the advanced practice role of nurse midwife;

2. Current certification as a nurse midwife from the American College of Nurse Midwives, or another nationally recognized certifying body which meets the requirements of Section VII of this Chapter; and

3. Written agreement with a consulting physician if providing intrapartum care.

## D. CLINICAL NURSE SPECIALIST (CNS)

1. Graduate degree evidencing successful completion of a nursing educational program, which shall include supervised clinical practice and classroom instruction in a nursing clinical practice specialty; and

2. Current certification in a specialty role as a clinical nurse specialist from a nationally recognized certifying body which meets the requirements of Section VII of this Chapter.

### SECTION III
### LICENSURE

## A. ELIGIBILITY
The applicant shall meet the licensure requirements of the Board.

## B. APPLICATION FOR LICENSURE BY EXAMINATION

In addition to a current registered nurse license to practice in Arkansas, the information submitted to the Board shall include:

1. A completed Board application form;

2. An official transcript or document from a nursing education program accredited by a nursing accrediting body that is recognized by the U.S. Secretary of Education and/or Council for higher Education Accreditation (CHEA), as acceptable by the Board and meets the qualifications of Section II of this Chapter in the category of advanced practice nursing for which the applicant is seeking licensure. The transcript or document shall verify the date of graduation, the degree or certificate conferred, clinical hours completed, and the role and population focus of the education program;

3. Evidence of state and federal criminal background checks conducted by the Arkansas State Police and the Federal Bureau of Investigation completed no earlier than twelve (12) months prior to the application for advanced practice licensure;

4. A statement directly from the Board approved national certifying body evidencing current certification in good standing; and

5. Payment of the nonrefundable fee.

## C. APPLICATION FOR LICENSURE BY ENDORSEMENT

1. The Board may issue a license by endorsement to an APN licensed under the laws of another state if, in the opinion of the Board, the applicant meets the qualifications for licensure in this state.

2. In addition to the requirements set forth in Section II and III.A. and B. of this Chapter, the information submitted to the Board shall include documentation of current unencumbered advanced practice licensure/authority to practice in another jurisdiction.

## D. APPLICATION FOR AN INTERNATIONALLY EDUCATED APN (educated outside theUnited States)

An internationally educated applicant for licensure in this state as an APN shall:

1. Graduate from a graduate level APN program equivalent to an APN educational program in the United States accepted by the board.

2. Submit an official transcript directly from the international nursing education program and verified through a qualified credentials evaluation process for the license being sought.

3. Meet all other licensure criteria required of applicants educated in the United States, including English proficiency.

## E. TEMPORARY PERMITS

1. Upon application and payment of the required fee, the Board shall issue a temporary permit to practice in an advanced practice nursing category to a qualified applicant who has no violations as listed in ACA § 17-87-312 on the Arkansas State Police criminal background check and:

a. Meets the educational requirements set forth in Section II of this Chapter and has been accepted by the appropriate certification body to sit for the first national certification exam he or she is eligible to take; or

b. Has a current advanced practice license or the equivalent from another jurisdiction and has current Board approved certification in the appropriate advanced practice nursing education category.

2. The temporary permit shall immediately become invalid upon receipt of information obtained from the federal criminal background check indicating any offense listed in ACA § 17-87-312 or upon notification to the applicant or ASBN of failure of the certification examination.

3. The temporary permit is not renewable and does not apply to prescriptive authority.

4. In no event shall the permit be valid in excess of six (6) months.

## F. RENEWALS

1. The date for renewal of licensure to practice as an advanced practice nurse shall coincide with renewal of the applicant's registered nurse license.

2. An applicant for renewal of an advanced practice nurse license shall submit to the Board:

a. A completed Board renewal application form;

b. Documentation of current national certification in the appropriate APN specialty through an maintenance program of a Board approved certifying body;

c. Documentation of current compact state RN licensure if primary state of residence has enacted the Interstate Nurse Licensure Compact; and

d. Payment of the nonrefundable renewal fee.

3. Advanced practice nurses with prescriptive authority shall submit evidence of a current collaborative practice agreement as a prerequisite to license renewal.

4. If disciplinary proceedings have been initiated against an individual with a lapsed, inactive, or retired license, the license shall not be renewed until the proceedings have been completed.

5. Continuing education submitted to the certifying body to meet the qualifications for recertification shall be accepted as meeting the statutory requirement for continuing education.

6. Upon request, an APN shall submit documentation to the Board of continuing education.

7. Effective January 1, 2010, APNs with prescriptive authority shall complete five (5) contact hours of pharmacotherapeutics continuing education in the APN's area of certification each biennium prior to license renewal.

## G. LAPSED LICENSE
The license is lapsed if not renewed or placed in an inactive status by the expiration date.

1. The license is lapsed if the RN license to practice in Arkansas is not renewed by the expiration date.
2. The license is lapsed when the national certification upon which licensure was granted expires.
3. Failure to receive the renewal notice shall not relieve the licensee of the responsibility for renewing the license by the expiration date.
4. Any licensee whose license has lapsed shall submit to the Board:
    a. A completed Board renewal application form;
    b. Documentation of current national certification; and
    c. The renewal fee and the reinstatement fee/late penalty.
5. Fees submitted to the Board are nonrefundable.
6. Any person engaged in advanced practice nursing during the time his or her license has lapsed shall be considered an illegal practitioner and shall be subject to the penalties provided for violation of the Nurse Practice Act.

## H. REINSTATEMENT OF APN LICENSE

1. An individual who applies for licensure reinstatement who has been out of practice for more than five years shall provide evidence of passing an APN nursing refresher course approved by the board or an extensive orientation in the appropriate advanced practice role and population focus which includes a supervised clinical component by a qualified preceptor who meets the following requirements:
    a. Holds an active unencumbered APN or physician license
    b. Is in current practice in the advanced role and population focus
    c. Functions as a supervisor and teacher and evaluates the individual's performance in the clinical setting
2. For those licensees applying for licensure reinstatement following disciplinary action, compliance with all board licensure requirements as well as any specified requirements set forth in the board's discipline order is required.

## I. INACTIVE STATUS

1. Any licensee in good standing who desires his or her advanced practice license to be placed on inactive status may submit a request in writing to the Board.
2. The APN license shall immediately be placed on inactive status when the registered nurse license is placed on inactive or retired status.
3. The current license shall be placed on inactive status upon receipt of the written request.
4. While the license is inactive, the licensee shall not engage in advanced practice

nursing nor be subject to the payment of renewal fees.

5. If the nurse desires to resume practice in this state, he or she shall request a renewal application, which shall be completed and submitted with a renewal fee and the reinstatement fee. Fees are nonrefundable.

6. All certification and continuing education requirements for renewal shall apply.

## J. RETIRED ADVANCED PRACTICE NURSE

1. Any advanced practice nurse in good standing whose registered nurse license has been placed on retired status may request that their APN license be placed on retired status.

2. The APN shall submit a request in writing, surrender the current license, and pay the required fee and the current license shall be placed on inactive status and a retired APN license issued.

3. An APN retired license shall be renewed biennially following submission of a renewal application and fee.

4. Fees are non-refundable.

5. While retired, the APN shall not practice nursing, however, an advanced practice nurse with a retired license may use the title "Advanced Practice Nurse" or the abbreviation "APN."

6. When the licensee desires to resume practice, he or she shall request a renewal application, which shall be completed and submitted with a reinstatement fee and the active renewal fee. The licensee must also meet those requirements outlined in Section III.E.

7. If the retired APN license is allowed to lapse, the licensee shall not hold himself or herself out as an APN and shall pay a reinstatement fee in addition to the fee required for renewal of the retired APN license.

## K. ADDITIONAL CERTIFICATIONS

1. An APN who has completed post-masters education for an additional nursing specialty shall:

   a. Submit a request for permission to practice in the new certification area;

   b. Submit a copy of authorization to sit for the first available certification exam from the Board approved certifying body;

   c. Immediately cease practicing in the specialty upon notification of failure of the exam;

   d. Submit results of the certification in the additional specialty directly from the certifying body;

   e. Submit an official transcript or document from a nursing education program that meets the qualifications in Section II of this Chapter verifying the date and degree or certificate conferred.

2. An APN who has prescriptive authority shall:

   a. Prescribe only for patients covered by the original specialty while waiting additional specialty results.

        b. Submit a collaborative practice agreement which includes the additional certification.

<h2 style="text-align:center">SECTION IV<br>DUPLICATE LICENSE</h2>

**A.** A duplicate license or certificate shall be issued when the licensee submits a notarized statement to the Board that the document is lost, stolen, or destroyed, and pays the required fee.

**B.** The license will be marked "duplicate".

<h2 style="text-align:center">SECTION V<br>NAME OR ADDRESS CHANGE</h2>

**A.** A licensee whose name is legally changed shall be issued a replacement license following submission of the current license, along with an affidavit, copy of marriage license or court action, and the required fee.

**B**. A licensee whose address changes from the address appearing on the current license shall immediately notify the Board in writing of the change.

<h2 style="text-align:center">SECTION VI<br>STANDARDS OF NURSING PRACTICE</h2>

**A. PURPOSE**

    1. To establish standards essential for safe practice by the advanced practice nurse.

    2. To serve as a guide for evaluation of advanced nursing practice.

**B. STANDARDS FOR ALL CATEGORIES OF ADVANCED PRACTICE NURS-**
**    ING**

    1. The advanced practice nurse shall assess clients at an advanced level, identify health status including abnormal conditions, establish a diagnosis, develop and implement treatment plans, and evaluate client outcomes.

    2. The advanced practice nurse shall use advanced knowledge and skills in teaching and guiding clients and other health team members.

    3. The advanced practice nurse shall use critical thinking and decision making at an advanced level, commensurate with the autonomy, authority, and responsibility of his/her practice category.

    4. The advanced practice nurse shall have knowledge of the statutes and rules

governing advanced nursing practice, and function within the legal boundaries of the appropriate advanced practice nursing category.

5. The advanced practice nurse shall recognize the APN's limits of knowledge and experience, planning for situations beyond expertise, and collaborating with or referring clients to other health care providers as appropriate.

6. The advanced practice nurse shall retain professional accountability for advanced practice nursing care when delegating interventions.

7. The advanced practice nurse shall maintain current knowledge and skills in the advanced practice nursing category.

8. Rules which apply to registered nurses are hereby incorporated by reference.

9. The APN shall comply with the standards for registered nurses as specified in Chapter I. Standards for a specific role and population focus of APN supersede standards for registered nurses where conflict between the standards, if any, exists.

**C.** In addition to the standards, the advanced practice nurse shall practice in accordance with the standards established by the national certifying body from which the APN holds his or her certification required for licensure. These standards shall have been reviewed and accepted by the Board.

## D. ADDITIONAL STANDARDS FOR CRNAs

1. The CRNA, acting in the normal course of his/her professional practice, may be authorized by a hospital or institution to act as their agent or employee to order the administration of controlled substances under the DEA registration of the hospital or institution.

2. The CRNA may order nurses to administer drugs preoperatively and/or postoperatively in connection with an anesthetic and/or other operative or invasive procedure that will be or has been provided.

3. The CRNA's order shall be directly related to the administration of drugs preoperatively and/or postoperatively in connection with an anesthetic and/or other operative or invasive procedure that will be or has been provided.

4. A CRNA who has not been granted authority by a DEA registrant as described in Title 21 CFR 1301.22, or its successor to order the administration of controlled substances shall give all orders as verbal orders from the supervising physician, dentist, or other person lawfully entitled to order anesthesia.

5. The CRNA shall be responsible for complying with all applicable state and federal laws and rules related to medications.

# SECTION VII
## PROFESSIONAL CERTIFICATION PROGRAMS

**A.** A national certification program which meets the following criteria shall be recognized by the Board to satisfy Section II of these rules.

**B.** The national certification program:

1. Is national in the scope of its credentialing;

2. Is accredited by a national accreditation body as acceptable by the Board;

3. Has no requirement for an applicant to be a member of any organization;

4. Has an application process and credential review which includes documentation that the applicant's education is in the advanced practice nursing category being certified, and that the applicant's clinical practice is in the certification category;

5. Education requirements are consistent with the requirements of the advanced practice role and population foci.

6. Uses an examination as a basis for certification in the advanced practice nursing category which meets the following criteria:

a. The examination is based upon job analysis studies conducted using standard methodologies acceptable to the testing community;

b. The examination represents entry-level practice in the APN role and population focus;

c. The examination represents the knowledge, skills, and abilities essential for the delivery of safe and effective advanced nursing care to clients;

d. The examination content and its distribution are specified in a test plan (blueprint), based on the job analysis study, that is available to examinees;

e. Examination items are reviewed for content validity and correct scoring using an established mechanism, both before use and periodically;

f. Examinations are evaluated for psychometric performance;

[g. omitted]

h. The passing standard is established using acceptable psychometric methods, and is reevaluated periodically;

i. Examination security is maintained through established procedures; and

j. A re-take policy is in place.

7. Issues certification based upon passing the examination and meeting all other certification requirements;

8. Provides for periodic recertification which includes review of continued education, qualifications, and continued competence;

9. Has mechanisms in place for communication to the Board for timely verification of an individual's certification status, changes in certification status, and changes in the certification program, including qualifications, test plan, and scope of practice;

10. Has an evaluation process to provide quality assurance in its certification program.

# SECTION VIII
## PRESCRIPTIVE AUTHORITY

## A. INITIAL APPLICANT
An applicant for an initial certificate of prescriptive authority shall:

    1. Be currently licensed as an advanced practice nurse in Arkansas.

    2. Provide evidence from the national certifying body that differential diagnosis and prescribing practices are recognized as being within the scope of practice for the applicant's certification category.

    3. Provide documentation of successful completion of pharmacology coursework which shall include pharmacokinetics principles and their clinical application and the prescription of pharmacological agents in the prevention and treatment of illness, and the restoration and maintenance of health.

    The coursework shall contain a minimum of:

        a. Three (3) graduate credit hour pharmacology course offered by an accredited college or university within two years immediately prior to the date of application to the Board; or

        b. Forty-five (45) contact hours [a contact hour is fifty (50) minutes] in a pharmacology course which includes a competency component, offered by an accredited college or university, within two (2) years immediately prior to the date of application to the Board; or

        c. Three (3) graduate credit hours pharmacology course, included as part of an advanced practice nursing education program, within five (5) years immediately prior to the date of application to the Board.

    4. Provide documentation of a minimum of three hundred (300) clock hours preceptorial experience in the prescription of drugs, medicines, and therapeutic devices with a qualified preceptor, to be initiated with the pharmacology course and to be completed within one year of the beginning of the course. Preceptorial experience completed as a part of the formal educational program in which the pharmacology course is taught will meet the three hundred (300) clock hour requirement.

    5. Submit a current collaborative practice agreement with a physician who is licensed under the Arkansas Medical Practices Act, § 17-95-201 et seq., and who has a practice comparable in scope, specialty or expertise to that of the advanced practice nurse. APN's who will prescribe controlled substances shall seek a collaborative practice with a physician who has an unrestricted DEA registration number. The collaborative practice agreement shall include, but not be limited to:

        a. Availability of the collaborating physician(s) for consultation or referral or both;

        b. Methods of management of the collaborative practice, which shall include the use of protocols for prescriptive authority;

        c. Plans for coverage of the health care needs of a client in the emergency absence of the advanced practice nurse or physician;

      d. Provision for quality assurance; and

      e. Signatures of the advanced practice nurse and collaborating physician(s), signifying mutual agreement to the terms of the collaborative practice.

6. Submit the nonrefundable processing fee with the application for a certificate of prescriptive authority.

## B. ENDORSEMENT APPLICANT

1. An applicant for endorsement of prescriptive authority shall:

      a. Provide documentation of a three (3) graduate credit hour pharmacology course offered by an accredited college or university or a forty-five (45) contact hour [a contact hour is fifty (50) minutes] pharmacology course which includes a competency component offered by an accredited college or university;

      b. Provide evidence that prescriptive authority is current and unencumbered in the jurisdiction from which the applicant is moving;

      c. Provide evidence of prescribing in a clinical setting for at least 500 hours in the year prior to application for a certificate of prescriptive authority;

      d. Have an unencumbered advanced practice nursing license to practice or the equivalent in the jurisdiction from which the applicant is moving;

      e. Provide a copy of current DEA registration (if prescriber has DEA number) and history of registration status; and

      f. Meet requirements in Section VIII.A.1,2,5,6.

2. Endorsement applicants who do not meet all requirements established herein shall be required to submit documentation acceptable to the Board according to Section VIII.A.

## C. PROTOCOLS FOR PRESCRIPTIVE AUTHORITY

Protocols shall be made available upon request of the Board. Such protocols shall, at a minimum, include:

1. Indications for and classifications of legend drugs, controlled substances (if prescriber holds a DEA registration number), and therapeutic devices which will be prescribed or administered by the APN;

2. Date the protocol was adopted or last reviewed, which shall be at least annually.

## D. PRESCRIBING PRIVILEGES

1. The APN, applying for a certificate of prescriptive authority, shall acknowledge in the application that he or she is familiar with all state and federal laws and rules regarding prescribing; and shall agree to comply with these laws and rules.

2. An advanced practice nurse with a certificate of prescriptive authority may receive and prescribe legend drugs, medicines, or therapeutic devices appropriate to the APN's area

of practice. The prescriptive authority for controlled drugs shall only extend to drugs listed in Schedules III through V.

3. Prescribing stipulations are as follows:

a. Legend drugs, therapeutic devices, and controlled substances (Schedules III-V), defined by the state and/or federal controlled substances lists, will be prescribed, administered, or ordered as established in protocols provided that the APN has an assigned DEA registration number which is entered on each written prescription for a controlled substance.

b. The APN shall file his/her DEA registration number with the Board upon receipt.

c. Advanced practice nurses shall not delegate to unlicensed ancillary staff the calling in of prescriptions to the pharmacy.

d. The APN shall notify the Board in writing the next working day following termination of the collaborative practice agreement. A new collaborative practice agreement is required to be on file prior to reactivating prescriptive authority.

4. The APN may prescribe a legend drug, medicine, or therapeutic device not included in the written protocols only as follows:

a. Upon a specific written or verbal order obtained from the collaborating physician before the prescription or order is issued by the APN; and

b. Include documentation of consultation as described above in the client's medical record to be signed by the APN;

c. Schedules I and II controlled substances shall not be prescribed under the APN's certificate of prescriptive authority.

5. The APN shall note prescriptions on the client's medical record and include the following information:

a. Medication and strength;

b. Dose;

c. Amount prescribed;

d. Directions for use;

e. Number of refills; and

f. Initials or signature of APN.

6. Advanced practice nurses in the category of certified registered nurse anesthetists shall not be required to have prescriptive authority to provide anesthesia care, including the administration of drugs or medicines necessary for such care.

7. Advanced practice nurses who prescribe prior to obtaining a certificate of prescriptive shall be considered illegal practitioners and shall be subject to the penalties provided for violation of the Nurse Practice Act.

## E. WRITTEN PRESCRIPTION FORMAT

1. All written prescriptions issued by the APN shall contain the name of the client, and the APN's name, telephone number, signature with the initials "APN", prescribing identification number issued by the Board, and should include information contained in Subsection D.5.a-f of this Section.

2. All prescriptions for controlled substances shall be written in accordance with federal rules. The APN's assigned DEA registration number shall be written on the prescription form when a controlled substance is prescribed.

## F. RECEIVING PREPACKAGED DRUG SAMPLES

1. APN's who have fulfilled requirements for prescriptive authority may receive legend drug samples and therapeutic devices appropriate to their area of practice, including controlled substances contained in Schedules III through V of the Controlled Substance Act, which have been prepared, packaged, or fabricated by a pharmaceutical manufacturer in accordance with the Arkansas pharmacy laws and rules.

2. Records must comply with all applicable federal and state laws and rules.

## G. TERMINATION OF PRESCRIPTIVE AUTHORITY

1. Prescriptive authority may be terminated by the Board when the prescriber:
    a. Fails to maintain current active licensure as an advanced practice nurse;
    b. Violates provisions of this Act and/or rules established by the Arkansas Department of Health, Nursing, or Pharmacy Boards;
    c. Violates any state or federal law or rules applicable to prescriptions; or
    d. Fails to follow any conditions imposed.

2. To reinstate prescriptive authority, the APN must meet requirements of the Board at the time of reinstatement.

## H. LAPSED CERTIFICATE OF PRESCRIPTIVE AUTHORITY

1. The certificate of prescriptive authority is lapsed if:
    a. The licensee's active advanced practice nurse license is not renewed by the expiration date;
    b. The national certification upon which licensure is based expires;
    c. There is not a current collaborative practice agreement on file with the board; or
    d. The advanced practice license is placed in inactive or retired status.

2. After reinstating a lapsed advanced practice license, the licensee shall submit to the Board a current collaborative practice agreement to reactivate the certificate of prescriptive authority.

3. Any person engaged in prescribing during the time his or her certificate of prescriptive authority has lapsed shall be considered an illegal practitioner and shall be subject to the penalties provided for violation of the Nurse Practice Act.

## I. INACTIVE STATUS

1. A certificate of prescriptive authority will automatically be considered lapsed and subject to the requirements of these rules when a licensee places his or her advanced practice license on inactive status.

2. While the certificate of prescriptive authority or advanced practice nurse license is inactive the licensee shall not engage in any practice within the scope of the certificate of prescriptive authority.

3. If the nurse desires to resume practice in this state, he or she shall request a renewal application which shall be completed and submitted with a renewal fee and the reinstatement fee. Fees are nonrefundable.

4. All certification requirements for renewal shall apply.

5. If disciplinary proceedings on an inactive licensee have been initiated, the license shall not be reinstated until the proceedings have been completed.

6. Effective January 1, 2010, APNs whose prescriptive authority is inactive shall complete five (5) contact hours of pharmacotherapeutics continuing education in the APN's area of certification for each 12 months of non-prescribing activity in addition to the five (5) contact hours required for APN license renewal prior to reactivation of prescriptive authority.

## SECTION IX
## PRESCRIPTIVE AUTHORITY ADVISORY COMMITTEE

### A. PURPOSE
The purpose of this committee shall include functioning in an advisory capacity to assist the Board with oversight and implementation of the provisions regarding prescriptive authority.

### B. COMPOSITION
The Advisory Committee shall be composed of five (5) members appointed by the Board and approved by the Governor. Three (3) members shall be advanced practice nurses holding certificates of prescriptive authority. One (1) committee member shall be a licensed physician who has been involved in a collaborative practice with a registered nurse practitioner for at least five (5) years. One member shall be a licensed pharmacist who has been in practice for at least five (5) years.

### C. TERMS OF OFFICE
Members shall serve three (3) year terms and may be reappointed. The Board may remove any advisory committee member, after notice and hearing, for incapacity, incompetence, neglect

of duty, or malfeasance in office.

## D. COMPENSATION

Advisory committee members shall serve without compensation; but may be reimbursed to the extent special monies are appropriated therefore for actual and necessary expenses incurred in the performance of their official Board duties.

## SECTION X
## NURSING EDUCATION PROGRAMS

### A.  NEW APN PROGRAM LEADING TO LICENSURE

1. Prerequisite Approval
   a. An institution, seeking to establish a new APN nursing education program leading to licensure, shall submit a letter of intent to the Board.
      (1) An applicant for an Advanced Practice Nursing (APN) program shall comply with the "Criteria and Procedures for Preparing Proposals for New Programs," established by the Arkansas Department of Higher Education.
      (2) Appropriate professional accreditation of the new APN program is considered to be deemed status as approved by the Board.
   b. The institution shall submit:
      (1) A copy of the curricula plan and course descriptions for Board review within thirty (30) days of sending the information to the accrediting body;
      (2) Other accreditation materials as requested by the Board; and
      (3) Documentation of accreditation within thirty (30) days of receipt of the report from the accrediting body.

### B. ESTABLISHED PROGRAM THAT PREPARES GRADUATES FOR LICENSURE

1. Continued Full Approval
   a. An established graduate program in advanced practice nursing shall submit to the Board documentation of the program's continued national nursing accreditation status within thirty (30) days of receipt from the accrediting body. Receipt of the documentation shall serve as deemed status for approval by the ASBN.

### C. EDUCATION PROGRAM

1. The education program for advanced practice nursing shall meet the nursing accrediting body standards for advanced practice nursing.

2. The curriculum plan for advanced practice nursing shall include:

    a. Preparation in one of the four identified APN roles (CRNA, CNM, CNS, and ANP); and

        b. Preparation in at least one of the approved population foci: (effective 2015)

            (1) Family/Individual Across the Lifespan

            (2) Adult-Gerontology

            (3) Neonatal

            (4) Pediatrics

            (5) Women's Health/Gender-related

            (6) Psychiatric/Mental Health; and

    c. Three separate graduate level courses (the APN Core):

        (1) Advanced physiology and pathophysiology

        (2) Advanced health assessment

        (3) Advanced pharmacology

3. Clinical Experiences

    a. All APNs who have a direct client care role, make diagnoses, prescribe therapeutic regimens and are accountable for these decisions shall have a minimum of 500 supervised clinical hours in direct clinical practice during the program.

    b. APN programs preparing for two population foci shall have a minimum of 500 supervised clinical hours for each population focus.

    c. Clinical supervision must be congruent with current national professional organizations and nursing accrediting body standards applicable to the APN role and population focus.

    d. Student clinical experiences shall be congruent with the population focus of the role.

[Effective July 1, 2010]

# CHAPTER FIVE
## DELEGATION

## A. PURPOSE

Registered nurses, licensed practical nurses, and licensed psychiatric technician nurses, within the parameters of their education and experience, are responsible for all nursing care that a client receives under their direction. Assessment of the nursing needs of a client, the plan of nursing actions, implementation of the plan, and evaluation of the plan, under the direction of a registered professional nurse, are essential components of nursing practice. Unlicensed personnel may be used to complement the licensed nurse in the performance of nursing functions; but such personnel cannot be used as a substitute for the licensed nurse. Delegation by registered nurses, licensed practical nurses, and licensed psychiatric technician nurses must fall within the definitions of Arkansas Code Annotated § 17-87-102. Delegation must occur within the framework of the job description of the delegatee and organizational policies and procedures, and must be in compliance with the Arkansas Nurse Practice Act. The following sections govern the licensed nurse in delegating and supervising nursing tasks to unlicensed personnel in all settings.

## B.  CRITERIA FOR DELEGATION

1. Delegation of nursing tasks to unlicensed persons shall comply with the following requirements:

a. A licensed nurse delegating the task is responsible for the nursing care given to the client and for the final decision regarding which nursing tasks can be safely delegated.

b. A licensed nurse must make an assessment of the client's nursing care needs prior to delegating the nursing task. (Ref. Section C. for exceptions.)

c. The nursing task must be one that a reasonable and prudent licensed nurse would assess to be appropriately delegated; would not require the unlicensed person to exercise nursing assessment, judgment, evaluation or teaching skill; and that can be properly and safely performed by the unlicensed person involved without jeopardizing the client's welfare.

d. A licensed nurse shall have written procedures available for the proper performance of each task and shall have documentation of the competency of the unlicensed person to whom the task is to be delegated.

e. The delegating licensed nurse shall be readily available either in person or by telecommunication.

f. The licensed nurse shall be responsible for documentation of delegated tasks.

g. Unlicensed nursing students may work only as unlicensed nursing personnel. They may not represent themselves, or practice, as nursing students except as part of a scheduled clinical learning activity in the curriculum of a Board approved nursing program.

h. The licensed nurse shall adequately supervise the performance of delegated nursing tasks in accordance with the requirements of supervision which follow.

2. Supervision: The degree of supervision required shall be determined by the licensed nurse after an evaluation of appropriate factors involved, including, but not limited to, the following:

a. The stability of the condition of the client;

b. The training and capability of the unlicensed person to whom the nursing task is delegated;

c. The nature of the nursing task being delegated; and

d. The proximity and availability of a licensed nurse to the unlicensed person when performing the nursing task.

## C. SPECIFIC NURSING TASKS WHICH MAY BE DELEGATED WITHOUT PRIOR NURSING ASSESSMENT

By way of example, and not in limitation, the following nursing tasks are ones that are within the scope of sound nursing practice to be delegated, provided the delegation is in compliance with ACA §17-87-102 and the level of supervision required is determined by the nurse.

1. Noninvasive and non-sterile treatments unless otherwise prohibited by Section D. of this Chapter (relating to nursing tasks that may not be routinely delegated);
2. The collecting, reporting, and documentation of data including, but not limited to:
   a. Vital signs, height, weight, intake and output, urine test, and hematest results;
   b. Changes from baseline data established by the nurse;
   c. Environmental and safety situations;
   d. Client or family comments relating to the client's care; and
   e. Behaviors related to the plan of care;
3. Ambulation, positioning, and turning;
4. Transportation of the client within a facility;
5. Personal hygiene;
6. Feeding, cutting up of food, or placing of meal trays;
7. Socialization activities;
8. Activities of daily living; and
9. Reinforcement of health teaching planned and/or provided by the registered nurse.

## D. NURSING TASKS THAT MAY NOT BE ROUTINELY DELEGATED

1. Nursing tasks not included in Section C. are not usually within the scope of sound nursing judgment to delegate and may be delegated only in accordance with subsection 2. of this section.
2. The nursing tasks of this section may be delegated to an unlicensed person only:
   a. Under circumstances where a reasonable and prudent licensed nurse would find that the delegation does not jeopardize the client's safety and/or welfare;
   b. If, in the judgment of the licensed nurse, the unlicensed person has the appropriate knowledge and skills to perform the nursing task(s) in a safe and effective manner;
   c. If the licensed nurse delegating the task is directly responsible for the nursing care given to the client;
   d. If the agency, facility, or institution, employing unlicensed personnel, follows a current protocol for the instruction and training of unlicensed personnel performing nursing tasks under this subsection; and that said protocol is developed by and taught under the supervision of registered nurses currently employed in the facility, and includes:
      (1) The manner in which the instruction addresses the complexity of the delegated task;

103

(2) The manner in which the unlicensed person demonstrates competency of the delegated task;

(3) The mechanism for reevaluation of the competency; and

(4) An established mechanism for identifying those individuals to whom nursing tasks under this subsection may be delegated; and

e. If the protocol recognizes that the final decision as to what nursing tasks can be safely delegated in any specific situation is within the specific scope of the nurse's professional judgment.

## E. NURSING TASKS THAT SHALL NOT BE DELEGATED

By way of example, and not in limitation, the following are nursing tasks that are not within the scope of sound nursing judgment to delegate:

1. Physical, psychological, and social assessment which requires nursing judgment, intervention, referral, or follow-up;

2. Formulation of the plan of nursing care and evaluation of the client's response to the care rendered;

3. Specific tasks involved in the implementation of the plan of care which require nursing judgment or intervention;

4. The responsibility and accountability for client health teaching and health counseling which promotes client education and involves the client's significant others in accomplishing health goals; and

5. Administration of any medications or intravenous therapy, including blood or blood products except as allowed by ASBN Rules Chapter 8 for Medication Assistant-Certified and by ASBN School Nurse Roles and Responsibilities Practice Guidelines.

6. Receiving or transmitting verbal or telephone orders;

7. Registered nurse practitioners and advanced practice nurses shall not delegate to unlicensed ancillary staff the calling in of prescriptions to the pharmacy.

## F. TRANSFERENCE OF DELEGATED NURSING TASKS

It is the responsibility of the licensed nurse to assess each client prior to delegation of a nursing task and determine that the unlicensed person has the competence to perform the nursing task in that client's situation.

1. The licensed nurse shall not transfer delegated tasks to other clients under the care of the unlicensed person.

2. In delegating personal care, a licensed nurse is not required to assess each client; but must periodically assess the competence of the caregiver in those activities.

## G. EXCLUSIONS

These sections shall not be construed to apply to:

1. The gratuitous nursing care of the sick by family or friends;

2. The furnishing of nursing care where treatment is by prayer or spiritual means alone;

3. Acts done by persons licensed by any board or agency of the State of Arkansas if such acts are authorized by such licensing statutes;

4. Nursing tasks performed by nursing students enrolled in Board approved nursing programs while practicing under the direct supervision of qualified faculty or preceptors;

5. The instruction and/or supervision of licensed nurses by registered professional nurses in the proper performance of tasks as a part of a state approved training/education course designed to prepare persons to obtain certification;

6. Nursing tasks performed by paramedic/emergency medical technician students enrolled in State approved programs while practicing under the direct supervision of qualified faculty or preceptors;

7. The performance in the school setting of nursing procedures necessary for students to achieve activities of daily living as cited in the Education of the Handicapped Act, 20 United States Code 1400-1485, and which are routinely performed by the student or the student•fs family in the home setting.

8. The acts of unlicensed persons responding to an emergency. This exclusion shall not be construed as permitting licensed nurses to delegate routinely to unlicensed persons.

9. Health maintenance activities performed by a designated care aide in the home as defined in the Consumer Directed Care Act of 2005, ACA § 17-87-103(11).

## H. CONSUMER DIRECTED CARE

1. Health maintenance activities may be provided by a designated care aide for a competent adult at the direction of the adult or for a minor child or incompetent adult at the direction of a caretaker.

2. Caretaker means a person who is directly and personally involved in providing care for a minor child or incompetent adult, and the parent, foster parent, family member, friend, or legal guardian of the minor child or incompetent adult receiving care.

3. Designated care aide means the person hired by the competent adult or caretaker to provide care for the competent adult, minor child, or incompetent adult.

4. Health maintenance activities mean activities that the minor child or adult is unable to perform for himself or herself.

5. The attending physician, advanced practice nurse, or registered nurse must determine a designated care aide under the direction of a competent adult or caretaker can safely perform the activity in the minor child's or adult's home.

6. Home shall not include nursing home, assisted living facility, residential care facility, an intermediate care facility, or hospice care facility.

7. Health maintenance activities that are not exempted by the Consumer Directed Care Act of 2005 include:

  a. Physical, psychological, and social assessment which requires nursing judgment, intervention, referral, or follow-up;

105

b. Formulation of the plan of nursing care and evaluation of the client•fs response to the care rendered;

c. Tasks that require nursing judgment or intervention;

d. Teaching and health counseling;

e. Administration of any injectable medications (intradermal, subcutaneous, intramuscular, intravenous, intraosseous, or any other form of injection) or intravenous therapy.

f. Receiving or transmitting verbal or telephone orders.

8. The designated care aide must demonstrate the ability to safely perform the health maintenance activity.

# CHAPTER SIX
## STANDARDS FOR NURSING EDUCATION PROGRAMS
[Note: Proposed changes to this Chapter immediately follow it]

## SECTION I
## APPROVAL OF PROGRAMS

This chapter presents the Standards established by the Arkansas State Board of Nursing for nursing education programs that lead to licensure.

## A. NEW PROGRAM LEADING TO LICENSURE

1. Prerequisite Approval

a. An institution, seeking to establish a new nursing program leading to licensure, shall submit a letter of intent to the Board.

(1) An applicant for a baccalaureate, diploma, associate degree, or practical nurse program shall comply with the approval process of appropriate state education approval authority.

(2) The parent institution shall be a post-secondary institution approved by the Arkansas Department of Higher Education or hospital approved by the Arkansas Department of health of a consortium of such institutions.

(3) Out of state nurse programs shall meet the requirements of the Arkansas Department of Higher Education and be approved by the Arkansas State Board of Nursing.

b. The institution must submit a current feasibility study, that is signed by the appropriate administrative officers, and includes the following:

(1) Purpose for establishing the program;

(2) Type of educational program to be established;

(3) Relationship to the parent institution, including an organizational

chart;

> (4) Mission, philosophy, purposes, and accreditation status of the parent institution;

> (5) Evidence that the parent institution has authorization or is in the process of obtaining authorization to conduct a program of nursing; or the approval status of parent institution;

> (6) Financial statement of the parent institution for the past two fiscal years;

> (7) A proposed budget for each year of the program's implementation;

> (8) Documented need and readiness of the community to support the program, including surveys of potential students, employment availability, and potential employers;

> (9) Source and numbers of potential students and faculty;

> (10) Proposed employee positions including support staff;

> (11) Proposed clinical facilities for student experiences, including letters of support from all major facilities expected to be used for full program implementation, including evidence of clinical space for additional students;

> (12) Letters of support from approved nursing and health-related programs using the proposed clinical facilities;

> (13) Proposed physical facilities including offices, classrooms, technology, library, and laboratories;

> (14) Availability of the general education component of the curriculum or letter of agreement, if planned, from another institution; and

> (15) A timetable for initiating the program, including required resources, and plans for attaining initial approval.

> (16) Other information as requested by the Board.

c. A representative of the Board shall conduct an on-site survey and complete a report.

d. The Board shall review all prerequisite documents during a regularly scheduled Board meeting.

e. The Board may grant, defer, or deny Prerequisite Approval.

f. After receiving Prerequisite Approval status, the institution may:

> (1) Advertise for students; and

> (2) Proceed toward compliance by following the Education Standards for Initial Approval.

2. Initial Approval

a. The institution shall secure a nurse administrator of the program.

b. The nurse administrator shall plan the program and

> (1) Assure compliance with Board standards and recommendations;

> (2) Address prerequisite recommendations;

> (3) Prepare detailed budget;

(4) Employ qualified faculty and support staff;

(5) Prepare a program organizational chart showing lines of authority;

(6) Design the program's sequential curriculum plan;

(7) Develop student, faculty, and support staff policies and procedures;

(8) Attain agency affiliation agreements;

(9) Verify that proposed physical facilities are in place; and

(10) Submit documentation to the Board that Initial Approval Standards are met.

c. A Board representative shall validate readiness of the program to admit students and prepare a report.

d. The Board shall review all documents for Initial Approval during a regularly scheduled Board meeting.

e. The Board may grant, defer or deny Initial Approval.

f. After receiving Initial Approval, the program:

(1) May admit students;

(2) Shall proceed toward compliance by following the Education Standards for Full Approval; and

(3) Shall follow the same standards as those of established programs in terms of annual activities, projects, and reports.

3. Full Approval

a. Before graduation of the first class, a Board representative shall validate compliance with the Standards and prepare a report.

b. The report and documentation shall be reviewed during a regularly scheduled Board meeting.

c. The Board may grant, defer, or deny Full Approval.

## B. ESTABLISHED PROGRAM THAT PREPARES GRADUATES FOR LICENSURE

1. Continued Full Approval

a. A survey will be periodically conducted to review the program for continued compliance with the Standards. An on-site or paper survey for a program includes:

(1) A newly established program shall have an on-site survey three (3) years after receiving initial Full Approval.

(2) An established professional or practical nurse program that has continued accreditation status with a national nursing accreditation organization and has maintained a NCLEXRN or NCLEX-PN pass rate of at least 75% shall have a paper survey every five (5) years thereafter.

(3) An established professional or practical nurse program that does not meet the criteria for accreditation with a national nursing education accreditation organization or has failed to maintain at least a 75% pass rate on the NCLEX-RN or NCLEX-PN shall have an onsite survey visit every five (5)

years thereafter.

b. The survey report and documentation shall be submitted to the Board and reviewed during a regularly scheduled Board meeting.

c. The Board may grant, defer, or deny Continued Full Approval.

2. Conditional Approval

a. If areas of noncompliance with standards are not corrected in the timeframe established by the Board, the Board shall award Conditional Approval.

b. Information regarding a nursing program requested by the Board shall be provided by the parent institution.

c. A representative of the Board shall conduct an on-site survey and complete a written report.

d. Additional information available to the Board may be considered.

e. The Board shall review all documents during a regularly scheduled Board meeting.

f. The Conditional Approval status shall be in effect for a maximum of one (1) year to correct noncompliance deviations from the standards, unless otherwise determined by the Board.

g. The program and parent institution shall receive written notification of noncompliance deviations and the Board action.

h. The Board may grant continued Conditional Approval, Full Approval, or withdraw the program's approval.

3. Satellite Campus

a. Satellite campus programs shall be approved by the Board prior to implementation.

(1) Continued Full Approval program may submit a proposal for a satellite campus program.

(2) The proposal shall reflect requirements for prerequisite approval of a new program.

b. The Board may grant, defer, or deny approval.

c. All approved satellite campus programs shall maintain the same standards as the parent program.

d. Each satellite campus' data will be included in the program's annual report and five-year survey report.

4. Distant Learning Sites

     a. Distant learning sites shall be approved by the Board prior to utilization.

     b. Each distant learning site's data shall be included in the program's annual report and five year survey report.

5. Out of state programs shall be Board approved prior to implementing clinical rotations in Arkansas healthcare facilities.


# SECTION II
# PROGRAM REQUIREMENTS

## A. ADMINISTRATION AND ORGANIZATION

1. Institutional Accreditation

     The parent institution shall be approved by the appropriate state body.

2. Institutional Organization

     a. The parent institution shall be a post-secondary educational institution, hospital, or consortium of such institutions.

     b. The institutional organizational chart shall indicate lines of authority and relationships with administration, the program, and other departments.

     c. The program shall have at least equal status with comparable departments of the parent institution.

3. Program Organization

     a. The program shall have a current organizational chart.

     b. The program shall have specific current job descriptions for all positions.

## B. PHILOSOPHY AND GRADUATE COMPETENCIES

1. The philosophy of the program shall be in writing and consistent with the mission of the parent institution.

2. Graduate competencies shall be derived from the program's philosophy.

3. The philosophy and graduate competencies shall serve as the framework for program development and maintenance.

## C. RESOURCES

1. Financial Resources

     a. There shall be adequate financial support to provide stability, development, and effective operation of the program.

     b. The director of the program shall administer the budget according to parent institutional policies.

     c. The director shall make budget recommendations with input from the faculty and staff.

2. Library and Learning Resource Center

    a. Each program and each satellite campus shall have a library or learning resource center with the following:

        (1) Current holdings to meet student educational needs, faculty instructional needs, and scholarly activities.

        (2) Budget plan for acquisitions of printed and multi-media materials.

        (3) Written process for identifying and deleting outdated holdings.

        (4) Resources and services accessible and conveniently available.

    b. The library of a baccalaureate, diploma, associate degree, or practical nurse program shall be under the direction of a qualified master's degree librarian.

## D. FACILITIES

1. Classrooms and Laboratories

    a. Each program and satellite campus shall have a clinical skills laboratory equipped with necessary educational resources.

    b. Classrooms and laboratories shall be:

        (1) Available at the scheduled time;

        (2) Adequate in size for number of students;

        (3) Climate controlled, ventilated, lighted; and

        (4) Equipped with seating, furnishings and equipment conducive to learning and program goals.

    c. Adequate storage space shall be available.

    d. Facilities shall be in compliance with applicable local, state, and federal rules and regulations related to safety and the Americans with Disabilities Act.

2. Offices

    a. The director of the program shall have a private office.

    b. Faculty members shall have adequate office space to complete duties of their positions and provide for uninterrupted work and privacy for conferences with students.

    c. There shall also be adequate:

        (1) Office space for clerical staff;

        (2) Secure space for records, files, equipment, and supplies; and

        (3) Office equipment and supplies to meet the needs of faculty and clerical staff.

3. Clinical Facilities

    a. Clinical facilities and sites shall provide adequate learning experiences to meet course objectives.

    b. Clinical sites shall be adequately staffed with health professionals.

    c. The program shall have a current and appropriate written agreement with each clinical site.

d. Written agreements shall include a termination clause and be reviewed annually.

e. Students shall receive orientation to each clinical site.

## E. PERSONNEL

1. Program Director

a. The program director shall have a current unencumbered registered nurse license to practice in Arkansas and be employed full time.

b. The practical nursing program director shall have a minimum of a baccalaureate degree in nursing. Directors appointed prior to January 1, 2004, shall be exempt for the duration of their current position.

c. The baccalaureate, diploma or associate degree program director shall have a minimum of a master's degree in nursing.

d. The program director shall have previous experience in clinical nursing practice and/or education.

e. The program director's primary responsibility and authority shall be to administer the nursing program.

(1) The program director shall be accountable for program administration, planning, implementation, and evaluation.

(2) Adequate time shall be allowed for relevant administrative duties and responsibilities.

f. The licensure examination application shall be authorized by the nursing program director to assure the applicant has completed the program.

2. Faculty and Assistant Clinical Instructors

a. Faculty shall hold a current unencumbered registered nurse license to practice in Arkansas.

b. Faculty shall have had previous experience in clinical nursing.

c. Faculty teaching in a baccalaureate, diploma, associate degree, or practical nurse program shall have a degree or diploma above the type of education program offered.

d. Nurses serving as assistant clinical instructors in a baccalaureate, diploma, associate degree, or practical nurse program may have a degree or diploma at or above the type of education program offered.

e. Assistant clinical instructors shall:

(1) Be under the direction of faculty;

(2) Hold a current unencumbered license to practice in Arkansas; and

(3) Have a minimum of one year experience in the clinical area.

f. All faculty shall maintain education and clinical competencies in areas of instructional responsibilities.

g. Non-nurse faculty shall meet the requirements of the parent institution.

h. Faculty shall be organized with written policies, procedures, and, if appropriate, standing committees.

      i. Nursing faculty policies shall be consistent with parent institutional policies.

      j. Program specific policies shall be developed by nursing faculty.

      k. A planned program specific orientation for new faculty shall be in writing and implemented.

      l. Consideration shall be given to safety, patient acuity, and the clinical area in determining the necessary faculty to student ratio for clinical experiences. The faculty to student ratio in clinical experiences shall be no greater than 1:10.

      m. The minimum number of faculty shall be one (1) full-time member in addition to the director.

      n. Faculty meetings shall be regularly scheduled and held. Minutes shall be maintained in writing.

      o. Faculty members shall participate in program activities as per policies and procedures.

3. Support Staff

      There shall be secretarial and other support staff sufficient to meet the needs of the program.

## F. PRECEPTORS

1. Preceptor Utilization

      a. Preceptors shall not be utilized in foundation or introductory courses.

      b. Preceptors shall not be considered in clinical faculty-student ratio. The ratio of preceptor to student shall not exceed 1:2.

      c. There shall be written policies for the use of preceptors, that include:

          (1) Communications between the program and preceptor concerning students;

          (2) Duties, roles, and responsibilities of the program, preceptor, and student; and

          (3) An evaluation process.

      d. All preceptors shall be listed on the annual report by area, agency, and number of students precepted.

2. Preceptor Criteria

      a. Baccalaureate, diploma, associate degree, or practical nurse program student preceptors shall hold a current unencumbered license to practice as a registered nurse in Arkansas. Practical nurse student preceptors shall hold a current unencumbered license to practice as a registered nurse, licensed practical nurse, or licensed psychiatric technician nurse in Arkansas.

      b. Preceptors shall have a minimum of one-year experience in the area of clinical specialty for which the preceptor is utilized.

      c. Preceptors shall participate in evaluation of the student.

3. Student Criteria

a. Precepted students shall be enrolled in courses specific to the preceptor's expertise.

b. Precepted students shall have appropriate learning experiences prior to the preceptorship.

c. There shall be no reimbursement to students for the educational preceptorship.

4. Faculty Criteria

a. Program faculty shall be responsible for the learning activity.

b. Program faculty shall be available for consultation with student and preceptor.

c. Program faculty shall be responsible for the final evaluation of the experience.

## G. STUDENTS

1. Admissions, Readmissions, and Transfers

a. There shall be written policies for admission, readmission, transfer, and advanced placement of students.

b. Admission criteria shall reflect consideration of potential to complete the program and meet standards to apply for licensure (See ACA §17-87-312).

c. Students who speak English as a second language shall meet the same admission criteria as other students and shall pass an English proficiency examination.

d. Documentation of high school graduation or an equivalent, as determined by the appropriate educational agency, shall be an admission requirement.

2. Progression and Graduation: There shall be written policies for progression and graduation of students.

3. Student Services

a. Academic and financial aid services shall be accessible to all students.

b. If health services are not available through the parent institution, a plan for emergency care shall be in writing.

c. There shall be provision for a counseling and guidance program separate from nursing faculty.

4. Appeal Policies: Appeal policies shall be in writing and provide for academic and non-academic grievances.

5. Program Governance: Students shall participate in program governance as appropriate.

## H. STUDENT PUBLICATIONS

1. Publications shall be current, dated, and internally consistent with parent institution and program materials.

2. The following minimum information shall be available in writing for prospective and

current students:

        a. Approval status of the program granted by the Board;

        b. Admission criteria;

        c. Advanced placement policies;

        d. Curriculum plan;

        e. Program costs;

        f. Refund policy;

        g. Financial aid information; and

        h. Information on meeting eligibility standards for licensure, including information on ACA § 17-87-312 and that graduating from a nursing program does not assure ASBN's approval to take the licensure examination.

3. The student handbook shall include the following minimum information:

        a. Philosophy and graduate competencies;

        b. Policies related to substance abuse, processes for grievances and appeal, grading, progression, and graduation; and

        c. Student rights and responsibilities.

## I. EDUCATIONAL PROGRAM

1. The education program shall include curriculum and learning experiences essential for the expected entry level and scope of practice.

        a. Curriculum development shall be the responsibility of the nursing faculty.

        b. Curriculum plan shall be organized to reflect the philosophy and graduate competencies.

        c. Courses shall be placed in a logical and sequential manner showing progression of knowledge and learning experiences.

        d. Courses shall have written syllabi indicating learning experiences and requirements.

        e. Theory content shall be taught concurrently or prior to related clinical experience.

        f. Clinical experiences shall include expectations of professional conduct by students.

        g. Curriculum plans for all programs shall include appropriate content in:

            (1) Introduction to current federal and state patient care guidelines;

            (2) Current and emerging infectious diseases;

            (3) Emergency preparedness for natural and man made disasters;

            (4) Impact of genetic research and cloning;

            (5) End of life care; and

            (6) Legal and ethical aspects of nursing, including the Arkansas Nurse Practice Act.

2. The curriculum plan for practical nurse programs shall include:

        a. Theoretical content and clinical experiences that focus on:

            (1) Care for persons throughout the life span including cultural

sensitivity;

        (2) Restoration, promotion, and maintenance of physical and mental health; and

        (3) Prevention of illness for individuals and groups.

    b. The length of the practical nurse curriculum shall be no less than ten (10) calendar months which includes at least thirteen hundred (1300) contact hours.

    c. Theory content may be in separate courses or integrated and shall include at least the following:

        (1) Anatomy and physiology;

        (2) Nutrition;

        (3) Pharmacology and intravenous therapy;

        (4) Growth and development throughout the life span;

        (5) Fundamentals of nursing;

        (6) Gerontological nursing;

        (7) Nursing of adults;

        (8) Pediatric nursing;

        (9) Maternal/infant nursing;

        (10) Mental health nursing; and

        (11) Principles of management in long term care, including delegation.

    d. Clinical experiences shall be in the areas of:

        (1) Fundamentals of nursing;

        (2) Nursing of adults;

        (3) Pediatric nursing;

        (4) Gerontological nursing;

        (5) Maternal/infant nursing;

        (6) Mental health;

        (7) Administration of medications, including intravenous therapy; and

        (8) Management in long term care, including delegation.

   3. The curriculum plan for baccalaureate, diploma, or associate degree nurse programs shall include:

    a. Theoretical content and clinical experiences that focus upon:

        (1) The prevention of illness and the restoration, promotion, and maintenance of physical and mental health;

        (2) Nursing care based upon assessment, analysis, planning, implementing, and evaluating; and

        (3) Care for persons throughout the life span, including cultural sensitivity.

    b. Course content may be in separate courses or integrated and shall include at least the following:

        (1) Biological and physical sciences content:

            a. Chemistry;

            b. Anatomy and physiology;

c. Microbiology;

d. Pharmacology;

e. Nutrition; and

f. Mathematics.

(2) Behavioral science and humanities content:

a. Psychology;

b. Sociology;

c. Growth and Development;

d. Interpersonal relationships;

e. Communication; and

f. English composition.

(3) Nursing science content:

a. Medical surgical adult;

b. Pediatrics;

c. Maternal/Infant;

d. Gerontology;

e. Mental Health;

f. Leadership, including nursing management and delegation; and

g. Baccalaureate programs shall include community health.

(4) Clinical experiences shall be in the areas of:

a. Medical/surgical;

b. Pediatrics;

c. Maternal/infant;

d. Mental health;

e. Gerontology;

f. Leadership and management, including delegation;

g. Rehabilitation; and

h. Baccalaureate programs shall include clinical in community health.

## J. PROGRAM EVALUATION

1. Faculty shall be responsible for program evaluation.

2. A systematic evaluation plan of all program aspects shall be in writing, implemented, and include: philosophy and graduate competencies, curriculum, policies, resources, facilities, faculty, students, graduates, and employer evaluation of graduates.

3. The outcomes of the systematic evaluations shall be used for ongoing maintenance and development of the program.

4. Appropriate records shall be maintained to assist in overall evaluation of the program after graduation.

5. The systematic program evaluation plan shall be periodically reviewed.

6. Students shall evaluate the courses, instructors, preceptors, and clinical experiences throughout the program, and the overall program after graduation.

## K. RECORDS

1. Transcripts of all students enrolled in the program shall be maintained according to policies of the parent institution.

    a. Transcripts shall reflect courses taken.

    b. The final transcript shall include:

        (1) Dates of admission;

        (2) Date of separation or graduation from the program;

        (3) Hours/credits/units earned, degree, diploma, or certificate awarded;

        (4) The signature of the program director, registrar, or official electronic signature; and

        (5) The seal of the school or be printed on security paper or an official electronic document.

    c. Current program records shall be safely stored in a secure area.

    d. Permanent student records shall be safely stored to prevent loss by destruction and unauthorized use.

## SECTION III
## REPORTS, LICENSURE EXAMINATION PERFORMANCE, AND CLOSURE

## A. REPORTS

1. Annual report: An annual report shall be submitted in a format and date determined by the Board.

2. Special reports/requests: The Board shall be notified in writing of major changes affecting the program, including but not limited to:

    a. School name;

    b. Director of Program; and

    c. Ownership or merger of parent institution.

3. Curriculum changes:

    a. Baccalaureate, diploma, associate degree, or practical nurse program changes – Major changes of curriculum or standards shall be reported to the Board prior to implementation, including but not limited to:

        (1) Philosophy, competencies, and objectives.

        (2) Reorganization of curriculum.

        (3) Increase or decrease in length of program.

    b. Practical Programs – Major changes of curriculum and standards shall be approved prior to implementation, including but not limited to:

(1) Philosophy, competencies, and objectives;

(2) Reorganization of curriculum; and

(3) Increase or decrease in length of program.

4. Pilot programs/projects that differ from the current approved program shall be approved prior to implementation.

## B. LICENSURE EXAMINATION PERFORMANCE

1. The student pass rate on the licensure examination shall be calculated on an annual calendar year.

2. The program shall maintain a minimum pass rate of 75% for first-time examination candidates.

3. Any program with a pass rate below 75% shall:

a. First year:

(1) Receive a letter of concern; and

(2) Provide the Board with a report analyzing all aspects of the program. The report shall identify and analyze areas contributing to the low pass rate and include plans for resolution which shall be implemented.

b. Second consecutive year:

(1) Receive a letter of warning; and

(2) Program director and parent institution representative shall present a report to the Board. The report shall identify and analyze the failure of first year corrections and additional plans for resolution of the low pass rate.

c. Third consecutive year:

(1) Be placed on conditional approval; and

(2) Conditional approval will be granted until two consecutive years of an above 75% pass rate is achieved or until the Board withdraws approval status for noncompliance with the education standards.

## C. PROGRAM CLOSURE

1. Voluntary

a. The parent institution shall submit a letter of intent for closure at least six (6) months prior to the closure. The letter shall include:

(1) Date of closure; and

(2) Plan for completion of currently enrolled students.

b. The Board must approve closure plan prior to implementation.

c. All classes and clinical experiences shall be provided until current students complete the program or parent institution provides for transfer to another acceptable program.

d. Records of a closed program shall be maintained by the parent institution and be in compliance with federal and state laws. The institution shall notify the Board of arrangements for the storage of permanent student and graduate records.

2. Mandatory

    a. Upon Board determination that a program has failed to comply with educational standards and approval has been withdrawn, the parent institution shall receive written notification for closure of the program. The notification shall include:

        (1) The reason for withdrawal of approval;

        (2) The date of expected closure; and

        (3) A requirement for a plan for completion of currently enrolled students or transfer of students to another acceptable program.

    b. Records of a closed program shall be maintained by the parent institution and be in compliance with federal and state laws. The institution shall notify the Board of arrangements for the storage of permanent student and graduate records.

3. A program that has had withdrawal of their approval status may apply as a new program after one year from official closure date.

Effective July 1, 2010

---

Proposed Changes to Chapter Six (additions underlined; deletions overstruck), and potential adoption date is unknown.

### CHAPTER SIX
### STANDARDS FOR NURSING EDUCATION PROGRAMS

SECTION I
APPROVAL OF PROGRAMS

This chapter presents the Standards established by the Arkansas State Board of Nursing for nursing education programs that lead to licensure.

A.  ~~NEW PROGRAM LEADING TO LICENSURE~~
    ~~1. Prerequisite Approval~~
      ~~a. An institution, seeking to establish a new nursing program leading to licensure, shall submit a letter of intent to the Board.~~
        ~~(1) An applicant for a baccalaureate, diploma, associate degree, or practical nurse program shall comply with the approval process of appropriate state education approval authority.~~
        ~~(2) The parent institution shall be a post-secondary institution approved by the Arkansas Department of Higher Education or hospital approved by the Arkansas Department of health of a consortium of such institutions.~~
        ~~(3) Out of state nurse programs shall meet the requirements of the Arkansas Department of Higher Education and be approved by the Arkansas State Board of Nursing.~~

A.  <u>New Program Leading to Licensure</u>
    <u>1. Institution Requirement</u>
      <u>a. An institution seeking to establish a new program of nursing shall meet the following requirements:</u>

        <u>(1). In- state educational institutions and consortiums seeking approval for a baccalaureate, diploma, associate degree, or practical nursing program shall be approved by the Arkansas Department of Higher Education and be accredited by accrediting body recognized by the United States Secretary of Education.</u>
        <u>(2) In-state hospitals or hospital consortiums shall be approved by the Arkansas Department of Health</u>

and accredited by the Joint Commission on Accreditation of Health Care Organizations.

(3) The proposed program must have an affiliation with a current State Board of Nursing approved program that is in good standing.

(4) The parent institution ~~will~~ shall meet the ~~requirements for~~ transfer or articulation requirements of ~~-courses in to other~~ Arkansas education institutions.

(b) Out of state programs shall meet the ASBN requirements for approval and ~~from with the~~ Arkansas Department of Higher Education. ~~and be approved by the Arkansas State Board~~

    B.   Prerequiste Approval

1. An institution seeking to establish a new nursing program leading to licensure shall submit a letter of intent to the Board at least one year prior to submission of proposal.

    a. The institution must submit a current feasibility study, that is signed by the appropriate administrative officers, and includes the following:

        (1)  Purpose for establishing the program;

        (2)  Type of educational program to be established;

        (3)  Copy of affliation agreement with current ASBN approved nursing program.

        (3)  Relationship to the parent institution, including an organizational chart;

        (4)  Mission, philosophy, purposes, and accreditation status of the parent institution;

        (5)  ~~Evidence that the parent institution has authorization or is in the process of obtaining authorization to conduct a program of nursing; or the approval status of parent institution;~~

        (6)  Financial statement of the parent institution for the past two fiscal years;

        (7)  A proposed budget for each year of the program's implementation;

        (8)  Documented need and readiness of the community to support the program, including surveys of potential students, employment availability, and potential employers;

        (9)  Source and numbers of potential students and faculty;

        (10) Proposed employee positions including support staff;

        (11) Proposed clinical facilities for student experiences, including letters of support from all major facilities expected to be used for full program implementation, including evidence of clinical space for additional students;

        (12) Letters of support from approved nursing and health-related programs using the proposed clinical facilities;

        (13) Proposed physical facilities including offices, classrooms, technology, library, and laboratories;

        (14) Availability of the general education component of the curriculum or letter of agreement, if planned, from another institution; and

        (15) A timetable for initiating the program through graduation of first class ~~;~~ includ~~ing~~ required resources, and plans for attaining full ~~initial~~ approval.

        (16) Other information as requested by the Board.

    a.   A representative of the Board shall conduct an on-site survey and complete a report.

    b.   The Board shall review all prerequisite documents during a regularly scheduled Board meeting.

    c.   The Board may grant, defer, or deny Prerequisite Approval.

    d.   If the Board denies Prerequisit Approval the program must wait two years before submitting another proposal.

    e.   …

…

## SECTION II
## PROGRAM REQUIREMENTS

A. ADMINISTRATION AND ORGANIZATION

    1.   Institutional Accreditation

        The parent institution shall be approved by the appropriate Arkansas state body.

    …

E. PERSONNEL

    1.   …

    2.   Faculty and Assistant Clinical Instructors

        a.   Faculty shall hold a current unencumbered registered nurse license to practice in Arkansas.

        b.   Faculty shall have had at least one previous experience in clinical nursing at or above the education level of the Institution.

...

l. Consideration shall be given to safety, patient acuity, and the clinical area in determining the necessary faculty to student ratio for clinical experiences. The faculty to student ratio in clinical experiences shall be no greater than 1:10~~0~~8.

...

3. Support Staff

There shall be secretarial designated ~~and other~~ support staff sufficient to meet the needs of the program.

...

I. EDUCATIONAL PROGRAM

1. The education program shall include curriculum and learning experiences essential for the expected entry level and scope of practice.

 j. Curriculum plans for all programs shall include appropriate content in:
 (1) Introduction to current federal and state patient care guidelines;
 (2) Current and emerging infectious diseases;
 (3) Emergency preparedness for natural and man made disasters;
 (4) Impact of genetic research on nursing care~~and cloning~~;
 (5) End of life care; and
 (6) Legal and ethical aspects of nursing, including the Arkansas *Nurse Practice Act.*

 ...

## SECTION III
### REPORTS, LICENSURE EXAMINATION PERFORMANCE, AND CLOSURE

C. PROGRAM CLOSURE

...

3. A program that has had withdrawal of their approval status may apply as a new program after ~~one~~ two years from official closure date.

_____

122

# CHAPTER SEVEN
## RULES OF PROCEDURE

### SECTION I
### ARKANSAS ADMINISTRATIVE PROCEDURE ACT

Rules, Rule Making, Notice of Hearing, Hearings, Judicial Review, Declaratory Orders, Adjudications, and other procedures authorized by the Arkansas Nurse Practice Act are governed by the Arkansas Administrative Procedures Act § 25-15-201 et seq.

### SECTION II
### PROCEDURE ON DENIAL, REPRIMAND, PROBATION, CIVIL PENALTIES, SUSPENSION, OR REVOCATION

#### A. GROUNDS FOR DISCIPLINE

1. The Board shall have sole authority to deny, suspend, revoke, or limit any license or privilege to practice nursing or certificate of prescriptive authority issued by the Board or applied for in accordance with the provisions of this chapter, or to otherwise discipline a licensee upon proof that the person:

   a. Is guilty of fraud or deceit in procuring or attempting to procure a license to practice nursing or engaged in the practice of nursing without a valid license;

   b. Is guilty of crime or gross immorality;

   c. Is unfit or incompetent by reason of negligence, habits or other causes;

   d. Is habitually intemperate or is addicted to the use of habit-forming drugs;

   e. Is mentally incompetent;

   f. Is guilty of unprofessional conduct;

   g. Has had a license, certificate or registration revoked, suspended, placed on probation, or under disciplinary order in any jurisdiction;

   h. Has voluntarily surrendered a license, certification, or registration, and has not been reinstated in any jurisdiction; or

   i. Has willfully or repeatedly violated any of the provisions of this chapter.

2. The board shall refuse to issue or shall revoke the license of any person who is found guilty of or pleads guilty or nolo contendere to any offense listed in ACA § 17-87-312(e) unless the person requests and the board grants a waiver pursuant to ACA § 17-87-312(g).

3. Proceedings under this section shall be as provided in the Arkansas Administrative Procedure Act, as amended, ACA § 25-15-201 et seq.

## B. PROCEEDINGS
Proceedings shall be as follows.

1. Opportunity for licensee or applicant to have hearing.

Except as provided in subsection 2 below, every licensee or applicant for a license shall be afforded notice and an opportunity to be heard before the Board. The Board shall have authority to take any action the effect of which would be to:

a. Deny permission to take an examination for licensing for which application has been duly made;

b. Deny a license after examination for any cause other than failure to pass an examination;

c. Withhold the renewal or reinstatement of a license for any cause;

d. Revoke a license;

e. Suspend a license;

f. Probate a license;

g. Reprimand a licensee;

h. Levy civil penalties.

2. Suspension of license without prior notice or hearing. If the Board finds that the continued practice by a licensee of the occupation or profession for which he or she is licensed will create an immediate hazard to the public, the Board may suspend the license pending a hearing without prior notice of hearing.

3. Notice of action or contemplated action by the Board-Request for Hearing-Notice of Hearing.

a. When the Board contemplates taking any action of a type specified in paragraphs a. and b. of subsection B.1. supra, it shall give written notice to the applicant at the last address of record in the Board office, including a statement:

(1) That the applicant has failed to satisfy the Board of his or her qualifications to be examined or to be licensed, as the case may be;

(2) Indicating in what respects the applicant has failed to satisfy the Board; and

(3) That the applicant may secure a hearing before the Board by depositing in the mail, within 20 days after service of said notice, a registered letter addressed to the Board containing a request for a hearing.

1. In any proceeding of the Board involving the denial of a duly made application to take an examination, or refusal to issue a license after an applicant has taken and passed an examination, the burden of satisfying the Board of the applicant's qualifications shall be upon the applicant.

2. When the Board contemplates taking any action of a type specified in subsections c, d, and e of subsection B.1. supra, it shall give a written notice to the licensee at the last address of record in the Board office, through the Board's attorney, which contains a statement:

(1) That the Board has sufficient evidence which, if not rebutted

or explained, will justify the Board in taking the contemplated action;

(2) Indicating the general nature of the evidence, and detailed allegations of violation of ACA § 17-87-309(a) (1-9) the licensee is charged with;

(3) That a hearing will be held on a date certain, no sooner than 20 days after the mailing of the notice to the last address of record in the Board office; and at that hearing the Board will receive evidence.

3. When the Board shall summarily suspend a license pending a hearing, as authorized in subsection B.2 supra, it shall give written notice of the general nature of the evidence and detailed allegations of violation of ACA § 17-87-309 (a)(1-9) the licensee is charged with:

(1) That the Board has sufficient evidence which, if not rebutted or explained, will justify revocation of the license by the Board;

(2) Indicating the general nature of the evidence against the licensee;

(3) That, based on the evidence indicated, the Board has determined that the continuation of practice of the occupation or profession of the licensee will create an immediate hazard to the public and has therefore suspended the license of the licensee effective as of the date such notice is served;

(4) The Board will then set an immediate hearing for a full evidentiary presentation by the licensee and the Board.

4. In any hearing before the Board involving the suspension or revocation of a license, the burden shall be on the Board to present competent evidence to justify the action taken or proposed by the Board.

## C. CIVIL PENALTIES

The Board may, after providing notice and a hearing, levy civil penalties in an amount not to exceed one thousand dollars ($1,000.00) for each violation against those individuals or entities found to be in violation of this Chapter or Rules promulgated thereunder.

1. Each day of violation shall be a separate offense.

2. These penalties shall be in addition to other penalties which may be imposed by the Board pursuant to this Chapter.

3. Unless the penalty assessed under this subsection is paid within fifteen (15) calendar days following the date for an appeal from the order, the Board shall have the power to file suit in the Circuit Court of Pulaski County to obtain a judgment for the amount of penalty not paid.

## D. ENCUMBRANCE OR SUSPENSION OF DEA REGISTRATION

The APN shall submit his/her DEA Registration to the Board upon request following disciplinary hearing in which the registration is encumbered or suspended.

## E. METHOD OF SERVING NOTICE OF HEARING

Any notice required by subsection B.3 above, may be served either personally or by an officer authorized by law to serve process, or by registered mail or certified mail with return receipt requested, directed to the licensee or applicant at his or her last known address as shown by the records of the Board. If notice is served personally, it shall be deemed to have been served at the time when the officer delivers the notice to the person addressed.

## F. VENUE OF HEARING

Board hearings held under the provisions of this rule shall be conducted at the Board office or elsewhere in Pulaski County.

## G. HEARINGS PUBLIC

Use of Hearing Office – All hearings under this section shall be open to the public. At all such hearings at least a quorum of the Board shall be present to hear and determine the matter.

## H. RIGHTS OF PERSONS ENTITLED TO HEARING

A person entitled to be heard pursuant to this section shall have the right to:

1. Be represented by counsel;
2. Present all relevant evidence by means of witnesses and books, papers and documents;
3. Examine all opposing witnesses on any matter relevant to the issues;
4. Have subpoenas and subpoenas duces tecum issued to compel the attendance of witnesses and the production of relevant books, papers and documents upon making written request therefore to the Board; and
5. Have a transcript of the hearing made at his or her own expense.

## I. POWERS OF THE BOARD IN CONNECTION WITH HEARING

In connection with any hearing held pursuant to the provisions of this section, the Board or its hearing officer shall have power to:

1. Have counsel to develop the case;
2. Administer oaths or affirmations to witnesses called to testify;
3. Take testimony;
4. Examine witnesses;
5. Have a transcript of the hearing made at the expense of the Board; and
6. Direct a continuance of any case.

## J. RULES OF EVIDENCE

In proceedings held pursuant to this rule, the Board may admit any evidence and may give probative effect to evidence that is of a kind commonly relied on by reasonably prudent men in the conduct of serious affairs. The Board may in their discretion exclude incompetent, irrelevant, immaterial, and unduly repetitious evidence.

## K. FEES – WITNESSES

Witness fees and mileage, if claimed, shall be allowed the same as for testimony in a Circuit Court.

## L. MANNER AND TIME OF RENDERING DECISION

After a hearing has been completed, the members of the Board shall proceed to consider the case and as soon as practicable shall render their decision. If the hearing was conducted by a hearing officer, the decision shall be rendered by the Board at a meeting where a quorum of the members of the Board is present and participating in the decision. In any case the decision must be rendered within ninety (90) days after the hearing.

## M. SERVICE OF WRITTEN DECISION

Within a reasonable time after the decision is rendered, the Board shall serve upon the person whose license is involved a written copy of the decision, either personally or by registered mail to the last address of record in the Board office. If notice is served personally, it shall be deemed to have been served at the time when the officer delivers the notice to the person addressed. Where notice is served by registered mail, it shall be deemed to have been served on the date borne by the return receipt showing delivery of the notice to the addresses or refusal to accept the notice. An attempt to serve notice at the last address of record shall constitute official notice.

## N. PROCEDURE WHERE PERSON FAILS TO REQUEST OR APPEAR FOR HEARING – REOPENING HEARING

If a person duly notified fails to appear for a disciplinary hearing and no continuance has been granted, the Board, or its hearing officer, shall hear the evidence of such witnesses as may have appeared, and the Board shall proceed to consider the matter and dispose of it on the basis of the evidence before it in the manner required by subsection L of Section II. Failure of the licensee to keep the Board informed of a change of address shall not be grounds to have the hearing reopened. Where because of accident, sickness, or other cause a person fails to appear for a hearing which has been scheduled by the Board, the person may, within a reasonable time, apply to the Board to reopen the proceeding; and the Board, upon finding such cause sufficient, shall immediately fix a time and place for hearing, and give such person notice thereof as required by Section II. At the time and place fixed, a hearing shall be held in the same manner as would have been employed if the person had
appeared in response to the original notice of hearing.

## O. CONTENTS OF DECISION

The decision of the Board shall contain:

1. Findings of fact made by the Board;
2. Conclusions of law reached by the Board;
3. The order of the Board based upon these findings of fact and conclusions of law; and
4. A statement informing the person whose license is involved of his right to request a

judicial review and the time within such request must be made.

# SECTION III
# ENFORCEMENT

## A. CIVIL ACTION
The Board may institute such civil suits or other legal proceedings as may be required for enforcement of any provisions of ACA § 17-87-101 through § 17-87-711 (Nurse Practice Act), as amended, and related acts.

## B. CRIMINAL ACTION
If the Board has reason to believe that any person has violated any provisions of the Nurse Practice Act, as amended, or related acts for which criminal prosecution would be in order, it shall so inform the prosecuting attorney in whose district any such purported violation may have occurred.

# SECTION IV
# DISCIPLINARY PROCEEDINGS

## A. DEFINITIONS

1. The term "fraud and deceit" shall include but not be limited to:
   a. False representation of facts on an application for licensure by examination or licensure by endorsement without examination or on application for renewal of license;
   b. False representation by having another person in his/her place for the licensing examination or any part thereof;
   c. Forged or altered documents or credentials as required for the application for original license, application for renewal of license, or application for certificate of prescriptive authority;
   d. Disclosing the contents of the licensing examination or soliciting, accepting, or compiling information regarding the examination before, during or after its administration;
   e. Aiding, abetting, assisting, or hiring an individual to violate or circumvent any law or duly promulgated rules intended to guide the conduct of a nurse or other health care provider;
   f. Prescribing any drug, medicine, or therapeutic device unless certified by the Board as having prescriptive authority.
   g. Engaging in the practice of nursing without a valid license.
2. The term "gross immorality" shall include but not be limited to acts and conduct inconsistent with the rules and principles of morality which relate to the practice of nursing and

the responsibilities of the licensee.

3. The term "negligence" means the failure to do some act of nursing which a licensee should do, guided by those ordinary considerations which regulate the practice of nursing; or the doing of something which a reasonable and prudent licensee would not do under the same or similar facts and circumstances in the practice of nursing. The term "gross negligence" is an exercise of such minimal care as to justify the belief that there was a conscious disregard or indifference for the health, safety, or welfare of the patient or the public and shall be considered a substantial departure from the accepted standard of care. The term "other causes" shall include but not be limited to the inability to practice nursing because of physical and/or psychological impairment.

4. The term "habitually intemperate or addicted" shall include but not be limited to the use of hallucinogenics, stimulants, depressants, or intoxicants which could result in behavior that interferes with the practice of nursing.

5. The term "mental incompetence" shall include those situations where a court has judged a licensee as incompetent.

6. The term "unprofessional conduct" includes, but is not limited to, the conduct listed below:

a. Failing to assess and evaluate a patient's status or failing to institute nursing intervention which might be required to stabilize a patient's condition or prevent complications.

b. Failing to accurately or intelligibly report or document a patient's symptoms, responses, progress, medications, and/or treatments.

c. Failing to make entries, destroying entries, and/or making false entries in records pertaining to the giving of narcotics, drugs, or nursing care.

d. Unlawfully appropriating medications, supplies, equipment, or personal items of the patient or employer.

e. Failing to administer medications and/or treatments in a responsible manner.

f. Performing or attempting to perform nursing techniques and/or procedures in which the nurse is untrained by experience or education, and practicing without the required professional supervision.

g. Violating the confidentiality of information or knowledge concerning the patient except where required by law.

h. Causing suffering, permitting or allowing physical or emotional injury to the patient or failing to report the same in accordance with the incident reporting procedure in effect at the employing institution or agency.

i. Leaving a nursing assignment without notifying appropriate personnel.

j. Failing to report to the Board within a reasonable time of the occurrence, any violation or attempted violation of the Arkansas Nurse Practice Act or duly promulgated rules or orders.

k. Delegating nursing care functions and/or responsibilities in violation of the Arkansas Nurse Practice Act and the Arkansas State Board of Nursing Rules, Chapter 5.

l. Failing to supervise persons to whom nursing functions are delegated or assigned.

m. Practicing nursing when unfit to perform procedures and make decisions in accordance with the license held because of physical, psychological, or mental impairment.

n. Failing to conform to the Universal Precautions for preventing the transmission of Human Immunodeficiency Virus and Hepatitis B Virus to patients during exposure prone invasive procedures.

o. Providing inaccurate or misleading information regarding employment history to an employer or the Arkansas State Board of Nursing.

p. Failing a drug screen as requested by employer or Board.

q. Engaging in acts of dishonesty which relate to the practice of nursing.

r. Failure to display appropriate insignia to identify the nurse during times when the nurse is providing health care to the public.

s. Failure to repay loans to the Nursing Student Loan Fund as contracted with the Board of Nursing.

t. Any other conduct that, in the opinion of the Board, is likely to deceive, defraud, injure or harm a patient or the public by an act, practice, or omission that fails to conform to the accepted standards of the nursing profession

.

7. The term "has had a license, privilege to practice, certificate, or registration revoked, suspended or placed on probation or under disciplinary order" refers to actions in any jurisdiction;

8. The term "has voluntarily surrendered a license, privilege to practice, certification, or registration and has not been reinstated" refers to actions in any jurisdiction.

9. The term "willfully" shall include but not be limited to:

a. Continuing action after notice by the Arkansas State Board of Nursing;

b. Disregarding the expiration date of the license;

c. Providing false, incorrect, or incomplete information to the employer regarding the status of the license;

d. Performing acts beyond the authorized scope of the level of nursing for which the individual is licensed, and practicing without required professional supervision;

e. Failing to follow the Nurse Practice Act of the State of Arkansas and its rules.

130

# CHAPTER EIGHT
## MEDICATION ASSISTANT-CERTIFIED

## SECTION I
## DEFINITION OF TERMS

**DESIGNATED FACILITY** – a nursing home.

**MEDICATION ASSISTANT-CERTIFIED – (MA-C)** – a person who is certified by the Board to administer certain nonprescription and legend drugs in designated facilities.

**SUPERVISION** – the oversight of the medication assistant-certified by a licensed nurse on the premises of a nursing home.

**LEGEND DRUG** – a drug limited by § 503(b)(1) of the federal Food, Drug, and Cosmetic Act to being dispensed by or upon a medical practitioner's prescription.

**INITIAL MEDICATION** – a new medication that the patient has not been receiving and/or changes in dosage, route, or frequency of a medication that a patient is currently receiving.

## SECTION II
## QUALIFICATIONS

**A.** In order to be certified as a medication assistant-certified, an applicant shall submit to the Arkansas State Board of Nursing written evidence, verified by oath, that the applicant:

    1. Is currently listed in good standing on the state's certified nurse aide registry;

    2. Has maintained registration on the state's certified nurse aide registry continuously for a minimum of one (1) year;

    3. Has completed at least one (1) continuous year of full-time experience as a certified nurse aide in this state;

    4. Is currently employed at a nursing home;

    5. Has a high school diploma or the equivalent;

    6. Has successfully completed a literacy and reading comprehension screening process approved by the Board;

    7. Has successfully completed a medication assistant-certified training course approved by the Board; and

    8. Has successfully passed a Board approved certification examination on subjects the Board determines; or

**B.** Has completed a portion of a nursing education program equivalent to the medication assistant person training course and passed the board's medication assistant certification and is otherwise qualified.

**C.** Any person holding certification as a medication assistant-certified shall have the right to use the title "medication assistant-certified" and the abbreviation "MA-C."

## SECTION III
## EXAMINATION

### A. ELIGIBILITY
The applicant shall meet the certification requirements of the Board.

### B. APPLICATION

1. Applications for examination shall be completed and filed with the Board prior to the examination.
2. Verification of successful completion of the medication assistant-certified program including date of completion shall be received in the Board office directly from the institution which provided the program.

### C. FEE

1. The examination fee shall accompany the application.
2. The examination fee (first time or retake) is not refundable.

### D. PASSING SCORE
The passing score on the certification examination shall be determined by the Board.

### E. FAILING SCORE AND ELIGIBILITY TO RETAKE THE EXAMINATION

1. Any applicant whose score falls below the passing score shall fail the examination.
2. The frequency and number of retests by unsuccessful candidates shall be determined by the Board.

### F. RESULTS
Examination results shall be available to all applicants and to their respective schools.

## SECTION IV
## MA-C IDENTIFICATION

**A.** Any person who holds a MA-C certification in this state shall use the legal title or abbreviation as set forth in Arkansas Code Annotated Section 17-87-101, et. seq. No other person shall assume any other name, title or abbreviation or any words, letters, signs, or devices that would cause a reasonable person to believe the user is certified as a MA-C.

**B.** Any person certified as a MA-C shall wear a name badge with name and appropriate legal title or abbreviation during times when such person is administrating medications.

**C.** The name badge shall be prominently displayed and clearly legible such that the person receiving medications may readily identify the type of personnel administering such medications.

# SECTION V
# SCOPE OF WORK

**A.** A MA-C may perform the delegated function of medication administration and related tasks under the supervision of a licensed nurse. A MA-C shall not administer any medication which requires nursing assessment or judgment prior to administration, evaluation and follow up, even if the medication is given by an approved medication route. A MA-C shall not administer medications to more than forty (40) patients during a shift.

## B. APPROVED MEDICATION ROUTES
The routes in which nonprescription and legend drugs may be administered by a MA-C when delegated by a licensed nurse include:

1. Orally
2. Topically
3. Drops for eye, ear or nose
4. Vaginally
5. Rectally
6. Transdermally
7. Oral inhaler

## C. TASKS NOT WITHIN THE SCOPE OF WORK
Tasks which shall not be delegated to the MA-C include, but are not limited to:

1. Receive, have access or administer controlled substances
2. Administer parenteral, enteral, or injectable medications
3. Administer any substance by nasogastric or gastrostomy tube
4. Calculate drug doses
5. Destroy medications
6. Receive written or verbal orders

7. Transcribe orders from the medical record
8. Order initial medications (Refer to Section I, Definition of Terms)
9. Evaluate medication error reports
10. Perform treatments
11. Conduct patient assessments or evaluations
12. Engage in patient teaching activities
13. Order or receive medications by a route that the medication assistant – certified can not administer.

## SECTION VI
## SUPERVISION

A licensed nurse shall not supervise more than two (2) medication assistant-certified persons during a shift.

## SECTION VII
## NURSING HOMES UTILIZING MA-C

Nursing homes utilizing MA-C persons shall notify the Board, on forms supplied by the Board. The notification shall be signed by the facility administrator and director of nursing.

## SECTION VIII
## DUPLICATE CERTIFICATE

**A.** A duplicate certificate shall be issued when the MA-C submits a statement to the Board that the document is lost, stolen, or destroyed, and pays the required fee.

**B.** The certificate will be marked "DUPLICATE."

## SECTION IX
## CERTIFICATION/VERIFICATION TO ANOTHER JURISDICTION

Upon payment of a certification/verification fee, a MA-C seeking certification in another jurisdiction may have a certified statement of Arkansas Certification issued to the appropriate entity in that jurisdiction.

## SECTION X
## NAME OR ADDRESS CHANGE

**A.** A MA-C whose name is legally changed, shall be issued a replacement certificate following submission of a notarized statement, copy of marriage license or court action, and the required fee.

**B.** A MA-C shall immediately notify the Board in writing of a change in mailing or residential address.

## SECTION XI
## RENEWALS

**A.** Each person certified under the provisions of ACA § 17-87-701 et. seq. shall renew certification biennially.

1. Thirty (30) days prior to the expiration date, the Board shall mail a renewal notification to the last known address of each MA-C to whom a certificate was issued or renewed during the current period.

2. An application shall be completed before the certification renewal is processed.

3. The certificate holder must attest to being currently listed in good standing on the state's certified nurse aide registry, have completed the required continuing education, and are currently employed.

4. The non refundable fee for renewal shall accompany the application.

5. Pursuant to Act 996 of 2003 and upon written request and submission of appropriate documentation, members of the Armed Forces of the United States who are Arkansas residents and are ordered to active duty to a duty station located outside of this state shall be allowed an extension without penalty or assessment of a late fee for renewing the service member's certification. The extension shall be effective for the period that the service member is serving on active duty at a duty station located outside of this state and for a period not to exceed six months after the service member returns to the state.

## B. EXPIRED CERTIFICATE

1. The certificate is expired if not renewed by the expiration date.

2. Failure to receive the renewal notice at the last address of record in the Board office shall notrelieve the MA-C of the responsibility for renewing the certificate by the expiration date.

3. Any MA-C whose certificate is expired shall file a renewal application and pay the current renewal fee and the late fee.

4. Any person practicing during the time the certificate has lapsed shall be considered to

be providing services illegally and shall be subject to the penalties provided for violation of ACA § 17-87-701 et seq.

5. When disciplinary proceedings have been initiated against a MA-C whose certificate has expired, the certificate shall not be reinstated until the proceedings have been completed.

6. A MA-C applying to reinstate an expired certificate to active status shall complete the continuing education requirements prior to reinstatement of the certificate and attest to being currently listed in good standing on the state's certified nurse aide registry.

7. If the expired period exceeds five (5) years, the person must repeat a medication assistant–certified personnel training program approved by the Board and successfully pass a Board approved certification examination.

## SECTION XII
## CONTINUING EDUCATION

Each person holding an active certificate or applying for reactivation of a certificate under the provisions as stated in these rules shall be required to complete certain continuing education requirements prior to certification renewal or reactivation.

### A. DECLARATION OF COMPLIANCE
Each MA-C shall declare his/her compliance with the requirements for continuing education at the time of certification renewal or reactivation. The declaration shall be made on the form supplied by the Board.

### B. REQUIREMENTS

1. A MA-C who holds an active certificate shall document completion of eight (8) contact hours of continuing education approved by Arkansas State Board of Nursing during each renewal period.

2. Expired certifications have no requirements for continuing education. Certification reactivation within two (2) years or less shall require documented completion of the following:

    a. Ten (10) contact hours of continuing education related to medication administration within the past two (2) years approved by the Arkansas State Board of Nursing, and

    b. Provide other evidence as requested by the Board.

3. Certification reactivation greater than two (2) years, but less than five (5) years shall require documented completion of the following;

    a. Ten (10) contact hours of continuing education related to medication administration within the past two (2)years approved by the Arkansas State Board of Nursing, or a medication related academic course, and

    b. Provide other evidence as requested by the Board.

4. Continuing education hours beyond the required contact hours shall not be carried over

to the next renewal period.

## C. RESPONSIBILITIES OF THE INDIVIDUAL CERTIFIED

1. It shall be the responsibility of each MA-C to select and participate in those continuing education activities that will meet the criteria.

2. It shall be the MA-C's responsibility to maintain records of continuing education as well as documented proof such as original certificates of attendance, contact hour certificates, academic transcripts or grade slips, and to submit copies of this evidence when requested by the Board.

3. Records shall be maintained by the MA-C for a minimum of two (2) consecutive renewal periods or four (4) years.

## D. RECOGNITION OF PROVIDERS

1. The Board shall approve all continuing education programs for the medication assistant-certified.

2. The Board shall work with the professional organizations, approved schools, and other providers of continuing educational programs to ensure that continuing education activities are available to MA-C's.

## E. ACTIVITIES ACCEPTABLE FOR CONTINUING EDUCATION

1. The educational activity shall be at least one (1) contact hour in length.

2. The content shall be medication related, relevant to the MA-C scope of work, and provide for educational growth.

3. If participation is in an academic course or other program in which grades are given, a grade equivalent of "C" or better shall be required, or "pass" on a pass/fail grading system.

## F. ACTIVITIES WHICH ARE NOT ACCEPTABLE AS CONTINUING EDUCATION

1. In-service programs. Activities intended to assist the MA-C to acquire, maintain, and/or increase the competence in fulfilling the assigned responsibilities specific to the expectations of the employer.

2. Orientation programs. A program by which new staff are introduced to the philosophy, goals, policies, procedures, role expectations, physical facilities, and special services in a specific work setting. Orientation is provided at the time of employment and at other times when changes in roles and responsibilities occur in a specific work setting.

3. Courses designed for lay people.

## G. INDIVIDUAL REVIEW OF A CONTINUING EDUCATION ACTIVITY PROVIDED BY A NONRECOGNIZED AGENCY/ORGANIZATION

1. A MA-C may request an individual review by:
   a. Submitting an "Application for Individual Review".
   b. Paying a fee.
2. Approval of a non-recognized continuing educational activity shall be limited to the specific event under consideration.

## H. AUDITS

1. The Board may perform random audits of MA-C's for compliance with the continuing education requirement.
2. If audited, the MA-C shall prove completion of the required continuing education during the twenty-four (24) months immediately preceding the renewal date, presenting photocopies of original certificates of completion to the Board.
3. MA-C shall provide evidence of continuing education requirements within thirty (30) calendar days from the mailing date of the audit notification letter sent from the Board to the last known address of the certified.
4. Certificate holders may be subject to disciplinary action by the Board if noncompliant with the audit.

## I. FAILURE TO COMPLY

1. Any MA-C who fails to complete continuing education or who falsely certifies completion of continuing education shall be subject to disciplinary action, non-renewal of the certificate, or both, pursuant to ACA §17-87-706 and ACA §17-87-707 (a)(1)(a) and (a)(5).
2. If the Board determines that a MA-C has failed to comply with continuing education requirements, the MA-C will:
   a. Be allowed to meet continuing education requirements within ninety (90) days of notification of non-compliance.
   b. Be assessed a late fee for each contact hour that requirements are not met after the ninety (90) day grace period and be issued a Letter of Reprimand. Failure to pay the fee may result in further disciplinary action.

## SECTION XIII
## ENDORSEMENT

**A.** The Board may issue certification as a MA-C by endorsement to an applicant who has been licensed or certified as a MA-C under the laws of another state or territory, regardless of title if:

1. In the opinion of the Board, the applicant meets the qualifications of MA-C in

this state; and
2. The Board recommends certification.

## B. APPLICATION

1. Applications must be completed, certified, signed by the applicant, and filed with the Board.
2. Endorsement verifications will be accepted from the state of original certification only.

## C. FEE

1. The endorsement fee must accompany the application.
2. The fees are not refundable.

# SECTION XIV
# STANDARDS FOR TRAINING PROGRAMS

## A. NEW PROGRAM APPROVAL

1. MA-C training programs shall be Board approved prior to implementation of the program.
2. The parent institution shall be a post secondary educational institution, hospital or consortium of such institutions which currently offers a nursing program, approved by the Board.
3. Approval
   a. The institution shall submit a proposal that is signed by the appropriate administrative officers, and includes:
      i. Evidence of adequate and appropriate faculty/resources to provide for the program and the requirements listed in this chapter.
      ii. A plan and timeline for meeting the program requirements.
   b. The Board shall conduct an initial survey
   c. The Board may grant, defer, or deny initial approval of the MA-C training program.
   d. After being granted approval, the institution may advertise and enroll students.

## B. ESTABLISHED PROGRAM APPROVAL

1. Continued Approval:
   a. A survey will be conducted every five (5) years to review the program for continued compliance with the Standards. The survey report and documentation shall be submitted to the Board and reviewed.

b. The Board may grant or defer continued approval or place the program on conditional approval.

2. Conditional Approval:

    a. If areas of non-compliance with standards are not corrected within the timeframe established by the Board, the Board shall award conditional approval.

    b. The conditional approval status shall be in effect for a maximum of one (1) year to correct noncompliance deviations from the Standards, unless otherwise determined by the Board.

3. The Board may grant continued conditional approval, full approval, or withdraw the MA-C training program's approval.

4. Satellite and Distance Learning sites shall be approved by the Board prior to implementation and shall meet the same standards as the parent program.

## C. PROGRAM REQUIREMENTS

1. Administration and Organization:

The parent institution shall be approved by the appropriate state body.

2. Financial Resources:

There shall be adequate financial support to provide stability, development and effective operation of the program.

3. Facilities:

    a. Each program and satellite campus shall have a clinical skills laboratory equipped with necessary educational resources.

    b. Classrooms and laboratories shall be:

        i. Available at the scheduled time.

        ii. Adequate in size for number of students.

        iii. Climate controlled, ventilated, lighted, equipped with seating, furnishings, and equipment conducive to learning and program goals.

    c. Adequate storage space shall be available.

    d. Facilities shall be in compliance with applicable local, state, and federal rules and regulations related to safety and the Americans with Disabilities Act.

    e. Offices:

        i. There shall be adequate office space for instructors.

        ii. There shall be secure space for records, files, equipment, and supplies.

        iii. There shall be office equipment and supplies to meet the needs of faculty and clerical staff.

    f. Clinical Facilities:

        i. Nursing homes shall provide adequate clinical learning experiences to meet course objectives.

        ii. Students shall receive orientation at each clinical site.

4. Personnel:

    a. The program shall have at least one instructor.

b. The instructor shall hold a current unencumbered registered nurse license to practice in Arkansas with at least two (2) years clinical experience and/or education experience in a nursing home.

c. The program may have clinical instructors who shall be licensed to practice nursing in Arkansas and have at least one (1) year recent experience in a nursing home.

d. An instructor or preceptor shall be onsite and available at all times during the student's clinical experience.

e. There shall be secretarial and other support staff sufficient to meet the needs of the program.

5. Students:

There shall be written policies for admission, readmission, progression, and completion for students which includes documentation of the student's qualifications which comply with ACA § 17-87-704.

6. Training Program:

a. The training program shall include curriculum and learning experiences essential for the expected entry level and scope of work of the MA-C.

b. The training program shall have at least one hundred (100) hours to include forty-five (45) hours of didactic study, fifteen (15) hours of skills lab practice, and forty (40) hours of supervised progressive clinical.

c. The didactic content shall include, but not be limited to:

    i. Role and scope of work of the MA-C;

    ii. The legal and ethical issues of medication administration;

    iii. Principles of medication properties, uses, and action;

    iv. Principles of medication administration including safety, infection control, communication, and documentation skills;

    v. Appropriate reporting of changes in clients' condition.

d. The skills lab shall include activities which focus on elderly clients in a nursing home.

e. Consideration shall be given to safety, patient acuity, and the clinical area in determining the necessary faculty to student ratio for clinical experiences.

f. The faculty to student ratio shall be no greater than 1:6

g. There shall be a supervised progressive clinical experience with the first twenty-four (24) hours under the direct supervision of the clinical instructor. A preceptor may supervise the remaining clinical hours.

7. Preceptors:

a. Preceptors shall be licensed to practice nursing in Arkansas and have at least one (1) year recent experience in a nursing home.

b. The ratio of preceptor to student shall not exceed 1:1.

c. There shall be written policies for the use of preceptors, that include:

    i. Communications between the program and preceptor concerning students.

    ii. Duties, roles, and responsibilities of the program, preceptor, and student.

    iii. An evaluation process.

d. All preceptors shall be listed on the annual report.

8. Program Evaluation:

a. Appropriate records shall be maintained to assist in overall evaluation of the program.

b. Students shall evaluate the courses, instructors, preceptors, and clinical experience.

9. Records:

a. Current program records shall be safely stored in a secure area.

b. The final record of all students enrolled in the program shall be maintained according to the policies of the parent institution.

c. The final record shall:

i. Reflect courses taken and include information as indicated by the Board;

ii. Be an official documentation of program completion;

iii. Be printed on security paper or an official electronic document.

d. Permanent student records shall be safely stored to prevent loss by destruction and unauthorized use.

## D. REPORTS, CERTIFICATION EXAMINATION PERFORMANCE, AND CLOSURE REPORTS

1. Reports:

a. An annual report shall be submitted in a format and date determined by the Board.

b. The Board shall be notified in writing of changes affecting the program, including but not limited to:

i. Curriculum

ii. School name

iii. Instructor

iv. Ownership or merger of parent institution

c. Curriculum and program changes shall be approved by the Board prior to implementation.

2. Certification Examination Performance:

a. The program shall maintain a minimum pass rate of 75% for first-time certification examination candidates.

b. Any program with an annual pass rate below 75% shall be required to submit a plan and a progress report which includes evaluation and implementation of changes to the program to achieve the minimum pass rate.

3. Program Closure:

a. Voluntary:

i. The parent institution shall submit a letter of intent and plan for closure at least six (6) months prior to the closure.

ii. The Board shall approve the closure plan prior to implementation.

iii. All classes and clinical experiences shall be provided until current students complete the program.

iv. Records of a closed program shall be maintained by the parent institution. The institution shall notify the Board of arrangements for the storage of permanent student and graduate records.

b. Mandatory:

i. Upon Board determination that a program has failed to comply with educational standards and approval has been withdrawn, the parent institution shall receive written notification for closure of the program. The notification shall include a requirement for a plan for completion of currently enrolled students or transfer of students to another acceptable program.

ii. Records of a closed program shall be maintained by the parent institution. The institution shall notify the Board of arrangements for the storage of permanent student and graduate records.

c. Reapplication of Training Programs:

i. A closed program may submit reapplication for a MA-C Training Program after two (2) years.

ii. Reapplication shall follow same procedure as initial program applicant.

## SECTION XV
## DISCIPLINE

## A. GROUNDS FOR DISCIPLINE

1. The Board shall have sole authority to deny, suspend, revoke, or limit any MA-C certification issued by the Board or applied for in accordance with the provisions of this chapter, or to otherwise discipline a MA-C upon proof that the person:

a. Has been found guilty of or pleads guilty or nolo contendere to:

i. Fraud or deceit in procuring or attempting to procure a MA-C certificate;

ii. Providing services as a MA-C without a valid certificate; or

iii. Committing a crime of moral turpitude.

b. Is unfit or incompetent by reason of negligence, habits, or other causes;

c. Is habitually intemperate or is addicted to the use of habit-forming drugs;

d. Is mentally incompetent;

e. Is guilty of unprofessional conduct;

f. Has had a certificate or registration revoked, suspended;

g. Has been placed on probation or under disciplinary order in any jurisdiction;

h. Has voluntarily surrendered a certification or registration and has not been reinstated in any jurisdiction; or

i. Has willfully or repeatedly violated any of the provisions of this chapter.

2. The Board shall refuse to issue or shall revoke the certification of any person who

would be disqualified from employment under the provisions of ACA §20-33-205.

## B. INVESTIGATIVE DETERMINATION, NOTICE OF FINDING

The Arkansas State Board of Nursing shall have jurisdiction to investigate all cases of suspected violation of ACA § 17-87-701 et. seq.

1. Upon completion of an investigation, the Arkansas State Board of Nursing shall determine that an allegation against a certificant is either:

a. Unfounded, a finding that shall be entered if the allegation is not supported by substantial evidence;

b. Founded, a finding that shall be entered if the allegation is supported by substantial evidence.

2. After making an investigative determination, the Arkansas State Board of Nursing shall provide notice of the following in writing to the certificant at the last known address of record:

a. The investigative determination;

b. The disciplinary action taken against the certificant;

c. Statement that the certificant with the founded report has the right to an administrative hearing upon a timely written request;

d. A statement that the written request for an administrative hearing shall be made to the Arkansas State Board of Nursing within thirty (30) days of receipt of the notice of determination.

e. The fact that the certificant has the right to be represented by an attorney at the certificant's own expense;

f. A statement that the certificant's failure to request an administrative hearing in writing within thirty (30) days from the date of receipt of the notice will result in submission of the investigative report, including the investigative determination, to all interested parties;

g. The consequences of a finding by substantial evidence through the administrative hearing process that violation of ACA §17-87-701 et seq has occurred.

## C. FINAL DETERMINATION OF FINDINGS

If the Arkansas State Board of Nursing's investigative determination of founded is upheld during the administrative hearing process or if the offender does not make a timely appeal for or waives the right to an administrative hearing, the Board shall report the final investigative determination in writing to all interested parties.

## D. SUBPOENAS AND SUBPOENAS DUCES TECUM

1. The Arkansas State Board of Nursing shall have the power to issue subpoenas and subpoenas duces tecum in connection with its investigations and hearings;

2. A Subpoena duces tecum may require any book, writing, document, or other paper or thing which is germane to an investigation or hearing conducted by the Board to be transmitted to the Board;

3. Service of subpoena shall be as provided by law for the service of subpoenas in civil

cases in the circuit courts of this state, and the fees and mileage of officers serving the subpoenas and of witnesses appearing in answer to the subpoenas shall be the same as provided by law for proceedings in civil cases in the circuit courts of this state;

4. The Board shall issue a subpoena or subpoena duces tecum upon the request of any party to a hearing before the Board;

5. The fees and mileage of the officers serving the subpoena and of the witness shall be paid by the party at whose request a witness is subpoenaed;

6. In the event a person shall have been served with a subpoena or subpoena duces tecum as provided in this section and fails to comply therewith, the Board may apply to the circuit court of the county in which the Board is conducting its investigation or hearing for an order causing the arrest of the person and directing that the person be brought before the court;

7. The court shall have the power to punish the disobedient person for contempt as provided by law in the trial of civil cases in the circuit courts of this state.

## E. CIVIL PENALTIES

The Board may, after providing notice and a hearing, levy civil penalties in an amount not to exceed one thousand dollars ($1,000.00) for each violation against those individuals or entities found to be in violation of this Chapter or Rules promulgated there under.

1. Each day of violation shall be a separate offense.

2. These penalties shall be in addition to other penalties which may be imposed by the Board pursuant to this Chapter.

3. Unless the penalty assessed under this subsection is paid within fifteen (15) calendar days following the date for an appeal from the order, the Board shall have the power to file suit in the Circuit Court of Pulaski County to obtain a judgment for the amount of penalty not paid.

## SECTION XVI
## ADVISORY COMMITTEE

**A.** The purpose of this committee shall include functioning in an advisory capacity to assist the Board with oversight and implementation of the provisions regarding medication assistant–certified.

## B. COMPOSITION

The Advisory Committee shall be composed of six (6) members appointed by the Board and approved by the Governor. Two (2) members shall be certified MA-C. One (1) member shall be a licensed nursing home administrator who has worked in that capacity for at least five (5) years of the last ten (10) years. One (1) member shall be a registered nurse who has been in a practice using certified nurse aides for at least five (5) years of the last ten (10) years. One (1) member shall be a lay person representing the interest of consumers of health care services. One (1) member shall be a registered nurse educator from an institution that offers a MA-C program.

## C. TERMS OF OFFICE

Members shall serve three (3) year terms and may be reappointed. The Board may remove any advisory committee member after notice and hearing for incapacity, incompetence, neglect of duty, or malfeasance in office.

## D. COMPENSATION

Advisory committee members shall serve without compensation, but may be reimbursed to the extent special monies are appropriated therefore for actual and necessary expenses incurred in the performance of their official Board duties.

# PART III
# POSITION STATEMENTS OF THE
# ARKANSAS STATE BOARD OF NURSING

## 94-1 Administration of IV Conscious Sedation by the Registered Nurse
Adopted November, 1994, Revised September 17, 2009

The Arkansas State Board of Nursing has determined that it is within the scope of practice of a registered professional nurse to administer pharmacologic agents via the intravenous route to produce moderate sedation. Consistent with state law, the attending physician or a qualified provider must order the drugs, dosages, and concentrations of medications to be administered to the patient. Optimal anesthesia care is best provided by qualified anesthesiologists and certified registered nurse anesthetists. However, the Board recognizes that the demand in the practice setting necessitates non-CRNA registered nurses providing IV conscious moderate sedation. A registered nurse may not administer medications that should be administered only by persons trained in the administration of general anesthesia. However, the administration of these medications for moderate sedation for comfort care in the final hours of life or for sedation of intubated critically ill patients is not prohibited.

As with all areas of nursing practice, the registered nurse must apply the *Nurse Practice Act* and Board *Rules* to the specific practice setting, and must utilize good professional judgment in determining whether to engage in a given patient-care related activity.

Employing facilities should have policies and procedures to guide the registered nurse. The Arkansas State Board of Nursing has adopted the attached guidelines.

## A.     Definition of Moderate Sedation

The American Society of Anesthesiologists (ASA) defines the various levels of sedation and anesthesia that are now incorporated into this statement. (ASA policy statement on Continuum of Depth of Sedation definition of General Anesthesia and Levels of Sedations/Analgesia, Approved by ASA House of Delegates on October 12, 1999, and amended on October 27, 2004.)

"Minimal Sedation" (Anxiolysis) is a drug-induced state during which patients respond normally to verbal commands. Although cognitive function and coordination may be impaired, ventilatory and cardiovascular functions are usually not affected. Appropriate medications for this purpose are benzodiazepines and opioids, but not anesthesia agents.

"Moderate Sedation" ("Conscious or Moderate procedural sedation") is a drug-induced depression of consciousness during which patients respond purposefully to verbal commands, either alone or accompanied by light tactile stimulation. No interventions are required to maintain a patent airway, and spontaneous ventilation is adequate. Cardiovascular function is usually maintained. Also, note that Procedural Sedation is also defined as the technique of administering sedatives or dissociative agents with or without analgesics to induce a state that allows the patient to tolerate unpleasant procedures while maintaining cardiorespiratory function. (American College of Emergency Physicians [ACEP], Clinical Policy for Procedural Sedation and Analgesia in the Emergency Department, Annals of Emergency Medicine, 2005.)

"Deep Sedation/Analgesia" is a drug-induced depression of consciousness during which patients cannot be easily aroused but respond purposefully following repeated or painful stimulation. The ability to independently maintain ventilatory function may be impaired. Patients may require assistance in maintaining a patent airway, and spontaneous ventilation may be inadequate. Cardiovascular function is usually maintained.

"General Anesthesia" is a drug-induced loss of consciousness during which patients are not arousable, even by painful stimulation. The ability to independently maintain ventilatory function is often impaired. Patients often require assistance in maintaining a patent airway, and positive pressure ventilation may be required because of depressed spontaneous ventilation or drug-induced depression of neuromuscular function. Cardiovascular function may be impaired.

## B.    Position Statement 94-1 Guidelines for Management and Monitoring

It is within the scope of practice of a registered nurse to manage the care of patients receiving IV moderate sedation during therapeutic, diagnostic, or surgical procedures provided the following criteria are met:
1. Administration of IV moderate sedation medications by non-anesthetist RNs is allowed by state laws and institutional policy, procedures, and protocol.
2. A qualified anesthesia provider or attending physician selects and orders the medications to achieve IV moderate sedation.
3. Guidelines for patient monitoring, drug administration, and protocols for dealing with potential complications or emergency situations are available and have been developed in accordance with accepted standards of anesthesia practice.
4. The registered nurse managing the care of the patient receiving IV moderate sedation shall have no other responsibilities that would leave the patient unattended or compromise continuous monitoring.
5. The registered nurse managing the care of the patient receiving IV moderate sedation is able to:
   a. Demonstrate the acquired knowledge of anatomy, physiology, pharmacology, cardiac dysrhythmia recognition and complications related to IV moderate sedation and medications.
   b. Assess total patient care requirements during IV moderate sedation and recovery. Physiologic measurements should include, but not be limited to, respiratory rate, oxygen saturation, blood pressure, cardiac rate and rhythm, and patient•f s level of consciousness.
   c. Understand the principles of oxygen delivery, respiratory physiology, transport and uptake, and demonstrate the ability to use oxygen delivery devices.
   d. Anticipate and recognize potential complications of IV moderate sedation in relation to the type of medication being administered.

e. Possess the requisite knowledge and skills to assess, identify and intervene in the event of complications or undesired outcomes and to institute nursing interventions in compliance with orders (including standing orders) or institutional protocols or guidelines.

f. Demonstrate skill in airway management resuscitation.

g. Demonstrate knowledge of the legal ramifications of administering IV moderate sedation and/or monitoring patients receiving IV moderate sedation, including the RN's responsibility and liability in the event of an untoward reaction or life threatening complication.

6. The institution or practice setting has in place an education/competency validation mechanism that includes a process for evaluating and documenting the individual•fs demonstration of the knowledge, skills, and abilities related to the management of patients receiving IV moderate sedation. Evaluation and documentation of competence occurs on a periodic basis according to institutional policy.

## C. Additional Guidelines

1. Intravenous access must be continuously maintained in the patient receiving IV moderate sedation.

2. All patients receiving IV moderate sedation will be continuously monitored throughout the procedure as well as the recovery phase by physiologic measurements including, but not limited to, respiratory rate, oxygen saturation, blood pressure, cardiac rate and rhythm, and patient's level of consciousness.

3. Supplemental oxygen will be immediately available to all patients receiving IV moderate sedation and administered per order (including standing orders).

4. An emergency cart with a defibrillator must be immediately accessible to every location where IV moderate sedation is administered. Suction and a positive pressure breathing device, oxygen, and appropriate airways must be in each room where IV moderate sedation is administered.

5. Provisions must be in place for back-up personnel who are experts in airway management, emergency intubation, and advanced cardiopulmonary resuscitation if complications arise.

## 95-1 Scopes of Practice
Adopted November 9, 1995, Revised May 15, 1998

The purpose of this position paper is to identify basic guidelines which may help nurses define and evaluate responsibilities and functions in relation to various types and scopes of nursing practice. The Board of Nursing does not intend to limit developing potentials of nursing practice by listing specific tasks, functions or responsibilities associated with all types and scopes of practice. When legal questions are raised, the Board will evaluate documentation that relates to the intent of the formal program of study and acceptance of practices by the nursing profession for that program. The profession of nursing is a dynamic discipline. Practice potentials change and develop in response to health care needs of society, technical advancements, and the expansion of scientific knowledge. All licensed nurses share a common base of responsibility and accountability defined as the practice of nursing. However, competency based practice scopes of individual nurses may vary according to the type of basic licensure preparation, practice experiences, and professional development activities.

Advanced licensure scopes of practice within nursing are also diverse. The profession of nursing generally recognizes that development of advanced practice occurs following the basic professional nursing education. Formal programs of study are designed to extend and expand upon basic registered nurse preparation. Such courses of study extend and expand the knowledge base of practice and provide for supervised practice in applying new knowledge in new ways.

The parameters of the practice scopes are defined by basic licensure preparation and advanced education. Within this scope of practice, all nurses should remain current and increase their expertise and skill in a variety of ways, e.g., practice experience, in-service education, and continuing education. Practice responsibility, accountability, and relative levels of independence are also expanded in this way.

It is the professional responsibility of each nurse to define their own career goals. Consistent with professional standards and regulations, each nurse has a responsibility to define and document an appropriate scope of nursing practice.

## GUIDELINES

1.  Educational programs that prepare nurses for basic licensure define the educational intent for the scope of basic practice. Changing curricula may expand the scope of practice of new graduates over time. Practicing nurses are expected to keep current with these changes through formal, continuing or inservice educational experiences. These experiences should be designed to evaluate and provide documentation of appropriate extensions of knowledge and practice.

2.  The advanced practice nurse shall practice in accordance with the scope of practice defined by the appropriate national certifying body and the standards set forth in the ASBN Rules and Regulations. The advanced practice nurse may provide health care for which the APN is educationally prepared and for which competence has been attained and maintained.

3.  The delivery of healthcare services which require assessment, diagnosis, intervention, and

evaluation fall within the professional nurse scope of practice.

4.  The delivery of healthcare services which are performed under the direction of the professional nurse, licensed physician, or licensed dentist, including observation, intervention, and evaluation, fall within the LPN/LPTN scope of practice.

5.  The nursing decision to carry out a health care act should always include consideration of:

    A.  Degree of immediate risk to the client if the action is not carried out when appropriate professional personnel are absent.

    B.  The overall complexity of the client's healthcare problem.

    C.  The degree of invasiveness of the act. The more invasive into the anatomical or physiological integrity of a client a task or activity is, the greater the liability of the nurse and the greater the risk to the public.

    D.  The reversibility of the action.

    E.  Prompt access to medical support.

    F.  The nurse's ability to prove by documentation and appropriate knowledge and skill base that the nurse is competent to perform the act.

## 95-2 Transmission and Acceptance of Verbal Orders
Adopted December 7, 1995

The Arkansas State Board of Nursing acknowledges that the best interests of all members of the health care team are served by having the licensed physician, licensed dentist, or advanced practice nurse holding a certificate of prescriptive authority write all orders on the patient's medical record. Although a licensed nurse relating verbal and telephonic orders to a licensed nurse may have become accepted practice, neither the Arkansas Nurse Practice Act nor the Arkansas State Board of Nursing Rules and Regulations specifically address this issue. Verbal orders transmitted over the phone place the licensed nurse at greater risk. Employing facilities should have policies and procedures to guide the licensed nurse.

However, the Rules and Regulations of the Arkansas State Board of Nursing do prohibit a licensed nurse from receiving or transmitting verbal orders to or from unlicensed personnel.

## 97-1 The Performance of Stapling, Suturing, or Application of Tissue Adhesive, for Superficial Wound Closure by Nurses in the Operating Room
Adopted March 13, 1997, Revised November 2001

### Statutory Definition

Arkansas Code Annotated § 17-87-102 defines "Practice of professional nursing" as: "... the performance for compensation of any acts involving the observation, care, and counsel of the ill, injured, or infirm; the maintenance of health or prevention of illness of others; the supervision and teaching of other personnel; the delegation of certain nursing practices to other personnel as set forth in regulations established by the Board; or the administration of medications and treatments as prescribed by practitioners authorized to prescribe and treat in accordance with state law, where such acts require substantial specialized judgment and skill based on knowledge and application of the principles of biological, physical, and social sciences".

"... the Practice of practical nursing" means the performance for compensation of acts involving the care of the ill, injured, infirm or the delegation of certain nursing practices to other personnel as set forth in regulations established by the board under the direction of a registered professional nurse, an advanced practice nurse, a license physician, or a licensed dentist, which acts do not require the substantial specialized skill, judgment, and knowledge required in professional nursing."

"Practice of psychiatric technician nursing" means the performance for compensation of acts involving the care of the physically and mentally ill, retarded, injured, or infirm or the delegation of certain nursing practices to other personnel as set forth in regulations established by the board, and the carrying out of medical orders under the direction of registered professional nurse, and advanced practice nurse, a licensed physician, or a licensed dentist, where such activities do not require the substantial specialized skill, judgment, and knowledge required in professional nursing."

### Position Statement

Numerous inquiries regarding the roles of nurses in the performance of stapling, suturing, or application of tissue adhesive has been received by the Arkansas State Board of Nursing. After study of the issues and concerns, the Arkansas State Board of Nursing issued the following position statement:

### Stapling and Suturing

The performance of stapling, suturing or application of tissue adhesive for superficial wound closure, as delegated by the attending surgeon in the operating room, is within the scope of nursing practice; however, the suturing of muscle, nerve, fascia, or tendon is not within the scope of their practice.

Nurses who perform stapling, suturing or application of tissue adhesive for superficial wound closure are responsible for having adequate preparation and experience to perform such acts and shall have documented competency with performance of such procedures. The nurse is responsible for documentation of educational preparation and for maintaining continuing competency.

In the performance of stapling, suturing, or application of tissue adhesive for superficial wound closure, the nurse should:

1) Have knowledge of the potential complications and adverse reactions, which may result from the procedure(s),
2) Have the knowledge and ability to recognize adverse reactions and to take appropriate nursing intervention as indicated, and
3) Perform the procedure(s) in accordance with the established written agency policies and procedures, which are consistent with the definition of "professional nursing practice", "practice of practical nursing," and "licensed psychiatric technician nurse" as stated in Arkansas Code Annotated § 17-87-102.

## Determining Scope of Practice

Arkansas Code Annotated § 17-87-309 and ASBN Rules, Chapter 7, Section IV, A.6.f., holds all nurses individually responsible and accountable for the individual's acts based upon the nurse's education and experience. Each nurse must exercise professional and prudent judgment in determining whether the performance of a given act is within the scope of practice for which the nurse is both licensed and clinically competent to perform.

## 97-2 Assistance with Self Medication for Unlicensed Persons
Adopted May 7, 1997

## DEFINITIONS

Assistance with Medication—Ancillary aid needed by an individual to self-administer oral medication, such as reminding the individual to take a medication at the prescribed time, opening and closing a medication container, returning a medication to the proper storage area, and assisting in reordering such medications from a pharmacy. Such ancillary aid shall not include calculation of medication dosage, or altering the form of the medication by crushing, dissolving, or any other method.

Setting—Location in which the purpose of the setting is other than the provision of health care such as an individual's residence which may include a group home or foster home as well as other settings including, but not limited to school, work or church where the individual participates in activities.

Cognitively Able—Awareness with perception, reasoning, intuition and memory.

Stable—A situation where the individual's clinical and behavioral status and care needs are nonfluctuating and consistent.

## POSITION

The Arkansas State Board of Nursing is authorized by ACA § 17-87-203 to regulate nurses, and nursing education and practice and to promulgate regulations in order to assure that safe and effective nursing care is provided by nurses to the public. Pursuant to ACA § 17-87-101, any person practicing nursing for compensation is required to hold nursing licensure. ACA § 17-87-102 allows the licensed nurse to delegate certain nursing practices to other personnel as set forth in regulations established by the board.

Effective September 25, 1995, the Board promulgated Chapter 5 of the Rules – titled *Delegation*. Delegation is defined in Chapter 1 as entrusting the performance of a selected nursing task to an individual who is qualified, competent and able to perform such tasks. The nurse retains the accountability for the total nursing care of the individual.

This position statement provides a guideline to nurses who supervise and delegate tasks to unlicensed persons who provide assistance in order to assure that care is provided in a safe and effective manner.

A licensed nurse shall not delegate to any unlicensed person the administration of medication. An unlicensed person is not precluded from assisting an individual with the self administration of oral medications in a setting where the purpose of the setting is other than the provision of health care.

Assistance with self medication by an unlicensed person may occur only as directed by physically impaired, cognitively able individuals with stable conditions. An unlicensed person assisting with the self administration of medication may only do the following:

(1)  Remind an individual when to take the medication and observe to ensure that the individual follows the directions on the container;

(2)  Assist an individual in the self administration of medication by taking the medication in its container from the area where it is stored and handing the container with the medication in it to the individual. If the individual is physically

unable to open the container, the unlicensed person may open the container for the individual; and

(3) Assist, upon request by or with the consent of, a physically impaired but cognitively able individual, in removing oral medication from the container and in taking the medication.

If an individual is physically unable to place a dose of oral medicine in the individual's mouth without spilling or dropping it, an unlicensed person may place the dose in another container and place that container to the mouth of the individual.

As set forth above, the assistance with self administration of oral medication shall not constitute the practice of nursing in a setting where the purpose of the setting is other than the provision of health care.

## 98-1 Administration of Analgesia by Specialized Catheter (Epidural, Intrathecal, Intra pleural)
Adopted March 14, 1998

The Arkansas State Board of Nursing has determined that, under the following conditions, it is within the scope of practice of the registered nurse, licensed practical nurse, and licensed psychiatric technician nurse to provide care to patients receiving analgesia by a specialized catheter.

**A. Catheter Placement, Initial Test Dosing, and Establishment of Analgesic Dosage Parameters.**

Placement of a catheter or infusion device, administration of the test-dose or initial dose of medication to determine correct catheter or infusion devise placement, and establishment of analgesic dosage parameters by written order for patients who need acute or chronic pain relief or for the woman during labor is to be done only by professionals who are educated and licensed in the specialty of anesthesia and physicians in other specialties who have been granted clinical privileges by the institution.

**B. Management and Monitoring**

1. In order for the nurse to manage the woman in labor who is receiving epidural analgesia, a qualified anesthesia provider must be within the facility. Only those RNs with education beyond licensure that is specific to obstetric analgesia may administer subsequent bolus doses and adjust the drug infusion rates according to the anesthesia provider's or physician's patient specific written orders.

2. A registered nurse (RN) may manage the care of patients with catheters or devices for analgesia to alleviate obstetrical labor pain, acute post surgical, pathological or chronic pain.

Management may include:
- a. Administration of a bolus dose through bolus feature of a continuous infusion pump, following establishment of appropriate therapeutic range;
- b. Adjustment of drug infusion rate in compliance with the anesthesia provider's or physician's patient-specific written orders;
- c. Replacement of empty infusion containers with new pre-prepared solutions;
- d. Stopping infusions;
- e. Initiating emergency therapeutic measures under protocol if complications arise;
- f. Removing the catheter upon written order;
- g. Accessing implanted ports with percutaneous access; and
- h. Monitoring the effectiveness of therapy and identification of complications.

3. A licensed practical nurse (LPN) or licensed psychiatric technician nurse (LPTN) may provide the care to patients with catheters or devices for analgesia to alleviate acute post surgical, pathological or chronic pain. Care may include:
- a. Replacement of empty infusion containers with new pre-prepared solutions
- b. Monitoring the effectiveness of therapy and identification of complications
- c. Stopping infusion

## C. Protocols, Education and Competency

It is within the scope of practice of the registered nurse, licensed practical nurse, or licensed psychiatric technician nurse to manage and/or provide the care of patients receiving analgesia by catheter as defined above only when the following criteria are met.
1. Management and monitoring of analgesia by catheter technique is allowed by institutional policy, procedure, or protocol.
2. The attending physician or the qualified anesthesia provider placing the catheter or infusion device selects and orders the medications, doses and concentrations of opioids, local anesthetics, steroids, alpha-agonists, or other documented safe medications or combinations thereof.
3. Guidelines for patient monitoring, medication administration and protocols for dealing with potential complications or emergency situations are available and have been developed in conjunction with the anesthesia or physician provider.
4. The registered nurse providing care for patients receiving analgesia by catheter or infusion device for acute or chronic pain relief or for the woman during labor is able to:
   - a. Demonstrate the acquired knowledge of anatomy, physiology, pharmacology and complications related to the analgesia technique (catheter and site specific) and medication.

b.   Assess the patient's total care needs during analgesia.

c.   Utilize monitoring modalities, interpret physiological responses and initiate nursing interventions to ensure optimal patient care.

d.   Anticipate and recognize potential complications of the analgesia in relationship to the type of catheter/infusion device and medication being utilized.

e.   Recognize emergency situations and institute nursing interventions in compliance with the anesthesia provider's or attending physician's guidelines and orders.

f.   Demonstrate the cognitive and psychomotor skills necessary for use of the analgesic catheter or mechanical infusion devices.

g.   Demonstrate knowledge and skills required for catheter removal.

h.   Demonstrate knowledge of the legal ramifications of managing and monitoring analgesia by catheter techniques, including the RNs responsibility and liability in the event of untoward reaction or life-threatening complication.

5.   The licensed practical nurse/licensed psychiatric technician nurse providing care for patients receiving analgesia by catheter or infusion device for acute or chronic pain relief or during labor is able to:

a.   Demonstrate the acquired knowledge of anatomy, physiology, pharmacology and complications related to the analgesia technique medication.

b.   Anticipate and recognize potential complications of the analgesia in relationship to the type of catheter/infusion device and medication being utilized.

c.   Recognize emergency situations and institute nursing interventions in compliance with the anesthesia provider's or attending physician's guidelines and orders.

d.   Demonstrate the cognitive and psychomotor skills necessary for use of the analgesic catheter or mechanical infusion devices.

6.   An educational/competency validation mechanism is developed, and documentation of the successful demonstration of knowledge, skills, and abilities related to the management of the care of persons receiving analgesia by catheters and pain control infusion devices for all nurses who will be providing such care is maintained by the institution. Education/competency validation is specific to type catheter, device and site being used. Evaluation and documentation of competence occurs on a periodic basis.

Adapted from the American Nurses Association's "Position Statement on the Role of the Registered Nurse (RN) In the Management of Analgesia by Catheter Techniques (Epidural, Intrathecal, Intrapleural, or Peripheral Nerve Catheters)" 1991.

**98-2  Insertion of Intrauterine Pressure Catheter**
Adopted May 14, 1998

The Arkansas State Board of Nursing has determined that it is not within the scope of practice of the registered nurse, licensed practical nurse, and licensed psychiatric technician nurse to insert intrauterine pressure catheters.


**98-6  Arkansas State Board of Nursing**
Approved: November 1998
Revised: January 1999

> *The mission of the Arkansas State Board of Nursing is to protect the public and act as their advocate by effectively regulating the practice of nursing.*

The profession of nursing is a dynamic discipline. Practice potentials change and develop in response to health care needs of society, technical advancements, and the expansion of scientific knowledge. All licensed nurses share a common base of responsibility and accountability defined as the practice of nursing. However, competency based practice scopes of individual nurses may vary according to the type of basic licensure preparation, practice experiences, and professional development activities.

The parameters of the practice scopes are defined by basic licensure preparation and advanced education. Within this scope of practice, all nurses should remain current and increase their expertise and skill in a variety of ways, e.g., practice experience, in-service education, and continuing education. Practice responsibility, accountability, and relative levels of independence are also expanded in this way.

The licensed nurse is responsible and accountable, both professionally and legally, for determining his/her personal scope of nursing practice. Since the role and responsibilities of nurses, and consequently the scope of nursing practice, is ever changing and increasing in complexity, it is important that the nurse makes decisions regarding his/her own scope of practice.

## THE PRACTICE OF NURSING

### The Practice of Professional (Registered) Nursing:

The delivery of health care services which require assessment, diagnosis, planning, intervention, and evaluation fall within the professional nurse scope of practice. The performance for compensation of any acts involving:

160

- the observation, care and counsel of the ill, injured or infirm;
- the maintenance of health or prevention of illness of others;
- the supervision and teaching of other personnel;
- the delegation of certain nursing practices to other personnel;
- administration of medications and treatments

where such acts require substantial specialized judgment and skill based on knowledge and application of the principles of biological, physical and social sciences. ACA § 17-87-102 (6)(A-E)

## The Practice of Advanced Practice Nursing:

The advanced practice nurse shall practice in accordance with the scope of practice defined by the appropriate national certifying body and the standards set forth in the ASBN Rules and Regulations. The advanced practice nurse may provide health care for which the APN is educationally prepared and for which competence has been attained and maintained. The delivery of health care services for compensation by professional nurses who have gained additional knowledge and skills through successful completion of an organized program of nursing education that certifies nurses for advanced practice roles as advanced nurse practitioners, certified nurse anesthetists, certified nurse midwives, and clinical nurse specialists. ACA § 17-87-102(4).

## The Practice of Registered Nurse Practitioner Nursing:

The delivery of health care services for compensation in collaboration with and under the direction of a licensed physician or under the direction of protocols developed with a licensed physician. ACA § 17-87-102(8)(A).

## The Practice of Practical Nursing:

The delivery of health care services which are performed under the direction of the professional nurse, licensed physician, or licensed dentist, including observation, intervention, and evaluation, fall within the LPN/LPTN scope of practice.

The performance for compensation of acts involving:

- the care of the ill, injured, or infirm;
- the delegation of certain nursing practices to other personnel under the direction of a registered professional nurse, an advanced practice nurse, a licensed physician or a licensed dentist, which acts do not require the substantial specialized skill, judgment, and knowledge required in professional nursing. ACA § 17-87-102 (5).

**The Practice of Psychiatric Technician Nursing:**

The performance for compensation of acts involving:

- the care of the physically and mentally ill, retarded, injured, or infirm;
- the delegation of certain nursing practices to other personnel the carrying out of medical orders under the direction of a registered professional nurse, an advanced practice nurse, a licensed physician or a licensed dentist, where such activities do not require the substantial specialized skill, judgement, and knowledge required in professional nursing. ACA § 17-87-102(7).

**Scope of Practice**
**Decision Making Model**
(on following page)

# SCOPE OF PRACTICE DECISION MAKING MODEL

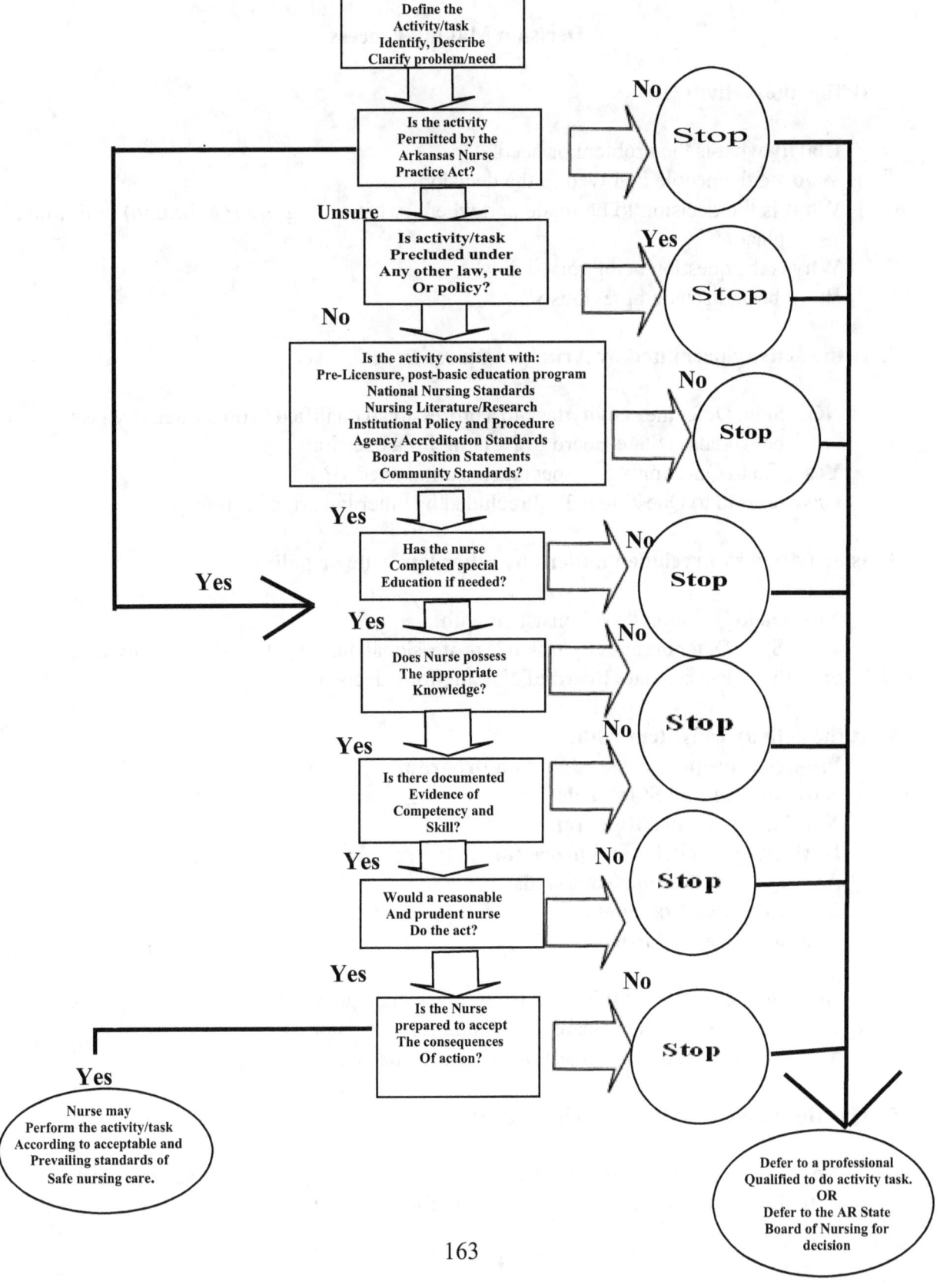

**Define the Activity/task Identify, Describe Clarify problem/need**

**Is the activity Permitted by the Arkansas Nurse Practice Act?** → No → **Stop**

Unsure

**Is activity/task Precluded under Any other law, rule Or policy?** → Yes → **Stop**

No

**Is the activity consistent with:**
Pre-Licensure, post-basic education program
National Nursing Standards
Nursing Literature/Research
Institutional Policy and Procedure
Agency Accreditation Standards
Board Position Statements
Community Standards? → No → **Stop**

Yes

**Has the nurse Completed special Education if needed?** → No → **Stop**

Yes

**Does Nurse possess The appropriate Knowledge?** → No → **Stop**

Yes

**Is there documented Evidence of Competency and Skill?** → No → **Stop**

Yes

**Would a reasonable And prudent nurse Do the act?** → No → **Stop**

Yes

**Is the Nurse prepared to accept The consequences Of action?** → No → **Stop**

Yes

**Nurse may Perform the activity/task According to acceptable and Prevailing standards of Safe nursing care.**

**Defer to a professional Qualified to do activity task. OR Defer to the AR State Board of Nursing for decision**

# Decision Making Process

## 1. Define the Activity/Task:

**Clarify** what is the problem or need?
**Who** are the people involved in the decision?
**What** is the decision to be made and where (what setting or organization) will it take place?
**Why** is the question being raised now?
Has it been discussed previously?

## 2. Is the activity permitted by Arkansas Nurse Practice Act?

**NO** – Stop. Defer the activity/task to a professional qualified to do the activity/task or to the Arkansas State Board of Nursing for a decision.
**Yes** – Go to Question # 5 – Special education needed?
**Unsure** – Go to Question # 3 – Precluded by other law, rule, or policy?

## 3. Is activity/task precluded under any other law, rule or policy?

**No** – Go to Question #4 – Consistent with….
**Yes** – Stop. Defer the activity/task to a professional qualified to do the activity/task or to the Arkansas State Board of Nursing for a decision.

## 4. Is the activity consistent with:
**Pre-licensure/post-basic education program**
**National Nursing Standards**
**Nursing Literature/Research**
**Institutional policies and procedures**
**Agency Accreditation Standards**
**Board Position Statements**
**Community Standards?**

**No** – Stop. Defer the activity/task to a professional qualified to do the activity/task or to the Arkansas State Board of Nursing for a decision.
**Yes** – Go to Question # 5 – Special education needs?

## 5. Has the nurse completed special education if needed?

**No** – Stop. Defer the activity/task to a professional qualified to do the activity/task or to the Arkansas State Board of Nursing for a decision.

**Yes** – Go to Question # 6 – Possess appropriate knowledge?

## 6. Does nurse possess appropriate knowledge?

**No** – Stop. Defer the activity/task to a professional qualified to do the activity/task or to the Arkansas State Board of Nursing for a decision.
**Yes** – Go to Question #7—Documented competency?

## 7. Is there documented evidence of competency & skill?

**No** – Stop. Defer the activity/task to a professional qualified to do the activity/task or to the Arkansas State Board of Nursing for a decision.
**Yes** – Go to Question #8 – Reasonable & prudent nurse?

## 8. Would a reasonable & prudent nurse perform the act?

**No** – Stop. Defer the activity/task to a professional qualified to do the activity/task or to the Arkansas State Board of Nursing for a decision.
**Yes** – Go to Question #9 – Prepared to accept consequences?

## 9. Is nurse prepared to accept the consequences of action?

**No** – Stop. Defer the activity/task to a professional qualified to do the activity/task or to the Arkansas State Board of Nursing for a decision.
**Yes** – Nurse may perform the activity/task according to acceptable and prevailing standards of nursing care.

### Guidelines for Decision Making

The nurse is constantly involved in the decision-making and problem solving process, whether as a staff nurse or a manager, regardless of the practice setting. Although their perspectives are different the process is the same. The following steps are basic to the process.

**Clarify**:

What is the problem or need?
Who are the people involved in the decision?
What is the decision to be made and where (what setting or organization) will it take place?
Why is the question being raised now?
Has it been discussed previously?

**Assess:**

What are your resources?
What are your strengths?
What skills and knowledge are required?
What or who is available to assist you?

**Identify Options:**

What are possible solutions?
What are the characteristics of an ideal
solution?
Is it feasible?
What are the risks?
What are the costs?
Are they feasible?
What are the implications of your decision?
How serious are the consequences?

**Point of Decision:**

What is the best decision?
When should it be done?
By whom?
What are the implications or consequences of your decision?
How will you judge the effectiveness of your decision?


## Application of Guidelines for Decision Making

**Clarify what it is you are being asked to do:**

- Gather facts that may influence the decision.
- Are there written policies and procedures available to describe how and under what conditions you will perform this task?
- Does the new responsibility require professional judgement or simply the acquisition of a new skill?
- Is this a new expectation for all RNs? LPNs? LPTNs?
- Has this been done before by others in your unit or health care facility?
- Is it just new to you?
- What about the other facilities in your community or region?
- What are the nurse manager• fs expectations about you or other RNs, LPNs,

LPTNs, becoming responsible for this procedure?
- When will this become effective?
- Will there be an opportunity to help you attain the needed clinical competency?
- Who will be responsible for the initial supervision and evaluation of this newly performed task?
- Will you be given additional time to learn the skill if you need it?

**Assess:**

- Are you clinically competent to perform this procedure?
- Do you currently have the knowledge and skills to perform the procedure?
- Have you had experience in previous jobs with this procedure?
- Who is available to assist you who has that skill and knowledge?
- Is that person accessible to you?
- Do you believe you will be able to learn the new skill in the allotted time?
- How can you determine that you are practicing within your scope of nursing?
- What is the potential outcome for the patient if you do or do not perform the procedure?

**Identify options and implications of your decision. The options include:**

- The responsibility/task is not prohibited by the Nurse Practice Act.

If you believe that you can provide safe patient care based upon your current knowledge base, or with additional education and skill practice, your are ready to accept this new responsibility.

You will then be ethically and legally responsible for performing this new procedure at an acceptable level of competency.

If you believe you will be unable to perform the new task competently, then further discussion with the nurse manager is necessary.

At this point you may also ask to consult with the next level of management or nurse executive so that you can talk about the various perspectives of this issue.

It is important that you continue to assess whether this is an isolated situation just affecting you, or whether there are broader implications. In other words, is this procedure new to you, but nurses in other units or health care facilities with similar patient populations already are performing? To what do you relate your reluctance to accept this new responsibility? Is it a work load issue or is it a competency issue?

At this point, it is important for you to be aware of the legal rights of your employer. Even though you may have legitimate concerns for patient safety and your own legal accountability in providing competent care, your employer has the legal right to initiate employee disciplinary action, including termination, if you refuse to accept an assigned task. Therefore, it is important to continue to explore options in a positive manner, recognizing that both you and your employer share the responsibility for safe patient care. Be open to alternatives. In addition, consider resources which you can use for additional information and support. These include your professional organization, both state and national, and various publications. The American Nurses Association Code for Nurses, standards on practice, and your employer's policies and procedures manuals are valuable resources. The Nurse Practice Act serves as your guide for the legal definition of nursing and the parameters that indicate deviation from or violation of the law.

**Point of decision/Implications.**
*Your decision maybe:*

**Accept** the newly assigned task. You have now made an agreement with your employer to incorporate this new responsibility, under the conditions outlined in the procedure manual. You are now legally accountable for its performance.

**Agree** to learn the new procedure according to the plans established by the employer for your education, skills practice and evaluation. You will be responsible for letting your nurse manager know when you feel competent to perform this skill. Make sure that documentation is in your personnel file validating this additional education. If you do not believe you are competent enough to proceed after the initial inservice, then it is your responsibility to let the educator and nurse manager know you need more time. Together you can develop an action plan for gaining competency.

**Refuse** to accept the newly assigned task. You will need to document your concerns for patient safety as well as the process you use to inform your employer of your decisions. Keep a personal copy of this documentation and send a copy to the nurse executive. Courtesy requires you also send a copy to your nurse manager. When you refuse to accept the assigned task, be prepared to offer options such as transfer to another unit (if this new role is just for your unit) or perhaps a change in work assigned tasks with your colleagues. Keep in mind though, when you refuse an assignment you may face disciplinary action, so it is important that you be familiar with your employer's grievance procedure.

## 99-1 Registered Nurse Deployment of Extravascular Collagen Plugs
Approved: January 14, 1999

The Arkansas State Board of Nursing has determined that, under the following conditions, it is within the scope of practice of the registered nurse to deploy extravascular collagen plugs for hemostasis.

1. Successful completion of an organized program of study which is approved by a nationally recognized accrediting body and provides didactic classroom instruction followed by supervised clinical practice which includes but is not limited to:
   a. Anatomy and physiology
   b. Patient screening
   c. Patient teaching
   d. Equipment
   e. Sterile technique
   f. Complication identification and management
   g. Documentation of pre/post teaching, procedure and follow-up
   h. Cognitive and psychomotor skills necessary to deploy an extravascular collagen plug
   i. Legal ramifications of deploying an extravascular collagen plug including the RN's responsibility and liability in the event of untoward reaction or life-threatening complications
   j. A mechanism for quality assurance and periodic review for competency
   k. Supervised clinical practice on a minimum of ten (10) successful deployments
2. Deployment of extravscular collagen plugs by RNs is allowed by institutional policy, procedure, or protocol.
3. A consent form designating the RN as the person performing the procedure is signed by the patient or their legally authorized representative.
4. A physician writes the order for the RN to deploy the extravascular collagen plug and is readily accessible to manage complications which may occur.
5. A periodic educational/competency validation mechanism is developed, and documentation of the successful demonstration of knowledge, skills, and abilities related to the management and care of persons receiving an extravascular collagen plug are on file for each nurse performing the procedure.

## 99-2 Delegated Medical Acts
Approved June 23, 1999

The definition of professional nursing found in the Arkansas State Board of Nursing Nurse Practice Act includes the administration of medications or treatments as prescribed by practitioners authorized to prescribe and treat in accordance with state law. In carrying out orders for the administration of treatments, RNs are engaged in the practice of professional nursing. However, in carrying out some physician orders, RNs may perform acts not usually considered to be within the scope of professional nursing practice. These tasks are delegated and supervised by physicians. This position statement provides guidance to the RN by clarifying the RN's responsibilities in carrying out delegated medical acts.

It is the Board's position that an RN may carry out the delegated medical act if the following criteria are met:

1.   The RN has received appropriate education and supervised practice, is competent to perform the procedure safely and can respond appropriately to complications and/or untoward effects of the procedure;
2.   The RN's education and skill assessment is documented in the RN's personnel record;
3.   The nursing and medical staffs have collaborated in the development of written policies/protocols/practice guidelines for the delegated acts and response to complications. These documents are available to nursing staff practicing in the facility and are reviewed annually;
4.   The procedure has been ordered by an appropriate licensed practitioner;
5.   Appropriate medical and nursing backup is available; and
6.   The delegated act is not prohibited by any other practice act, rule, regulation, or position statement (e.g., anesthetic agents, other than local anesthetics, can only be administered by the RN if he/she holds a CRNA license).

The Arkansas State Board of Nursing's document 98-6 entitled "Scope of Practice Decision Making Model" should be reviewed by the RN in conjunction with this position statement.


### 99-3 APNs Prescribing for Self & Family
Adopted: November 18, 1999

Prescribing controlled substances and other legend drugs for self and family raises many ethical questions. Prescribing for self and family members has inherent risks related to lack of objectivity. Effort should be made to discuss the condition with the collaborating physician. In addition, the Arkansas State Board of Nursing Rules and Regulations. Chapter Four. Section VIII.D.5. outlines the documentation requirements for prescribing.

The Arkansas State Board of Nursing has determined that the Advanced Practice Nurse with prescriptive authority may prescribe for self and family under the following circumstances:

1.   There shall be a medical record on the patient/client to document the prescription of the medication.
2.   The prescription must be within the prescribers scope of practice.
3.   The prescription shall be documented on the medical record in accordance with Arkansas State Board of Nursing Rules and Regulations. Chapter Four. Section VIII. D.3-5, portions of which are reprinted below:

The APN shall note prescriptions on the client's medical record and include the following information:

a. Medication and strength;
b. Dose;
c. Amount prescribed;
d. Directions for use;
e. Number of refills; and
f. Initials or signature of APN.

## 00-1 Administration of Medications and/or Treatments
Adopted: April 20, 2000

The Arkansas State Board of Nursing has determined that decisions regarding the administration of medications and/or treatments by the licensed nurse are governed by the Arkansas State Board of Nursing Scopes of Practice and Decision Making Model Position Statements. Arkansas State Board of Nursing Rules and Regulations:

The term "unprofessional conduct" is defined as conduct which, in the opinion of the Board, is likely to deceive, defraud, or injure patients or the public, means any act, practice, or omission that fails to conform to the accepted standards of the nursing profession and which results from conscious disregard for the health and welfare of the public and of the patient under the nurse's care; and includes, but is not limited to, the conduct listed below:

- Failing to administer medications and/or treatments in a responsible manner
- Performing or attempting to perform nursing techniques and/or procedures in which the nurse is untrained by experience or education, and practicing without the required professional supervision.

If the Board received a complaint regarding the administration of a medication and/or treatment, evidence would be collected regarding the nurse's actions. The nurse who administered the medication and/or treatment, may be required to show that his/her actions were consistent with current acceptable practice and that they had had the appropriate training, experience and/or education. Evidence may include, but is not limited to, manufacturer's literature, nursing journals, research articles, national organization position statements and standards of care and documentation of competency.

## 00-2 Telenursing
Adopted: November 16, 2000

Telenursing is defined as the practice of nursing using protocols through telecommunication technology. The Arkansas State Board of Nursing has determined that an active license to practice nursing in Arkansas is required to practice telenursing in this state. The ASBN "Position Statement 98-6 Decision Making Model" shall be followed to determine if a particular act of telenursing is within the scope of practice of the nurse, with emphasis on completion of special education, possession of appropriate knowledge, and documented evidence of competency and skill in the nurse's personnel file.

Health care professionals have been using various forms of telehealth for many years, and according to the American Nurses Association Core Principles of Telehealth (1999), the basic standards of professional practice are not altered by the use of telehealth technologies in the provision of health care.

It is further stated that, "A health care practitioner cannot use telehealth as a vehicle for providing services that are not otherwise legally or professionally authorized."

The practice of professional nursing (registered nursing) in the Arkansas State Board of Nursing Nurse Practice Act, ACA §17-87-102(6), means the performance of acts which require substantial specialized judgment and skill based on knowledge and application of the principles of biological, physical, and social sciences. Assessment is within the practice parameters of the RN in the ASBN "Position Statement 95-1 Scopes of Practice."

In ACA § 17-87-102(5) and (7), the practices of licensed practical nursing and licensed psychiatric technician nursing means the performance of acts under the direction of a registered professional nurse, an advanced practice nurse, a licensed physician, or a licensed dentist, those acts which "…do not require the substantial specialized skill, judgment, and knowledge required in professional nursing." Observation is within the practice parameters of the LPN/LPTN in the ASBN "Position Statement 95-1 Scopes of Practice."

The ASBN has determined that nurses licensed to practice in Arkansas may practice tele-nursing under the following circumstances:

1.  There shall be an established relationship with the client and a record to document data collected and all care provided or recommended.

2.  There shall be protocols that outline the care to be given. These protocols shall be reviewed annually by the licensed physician and nurse and be made available to the Board upon request.

3.  Documentation of each client contact shall include demographics, health history, assessment of the chief complaint, the protocol followed, referral, and, if indicated, any follow-up.

4.  Deviations from protocols shall require a direct order from a practitioner authorized to prescribe and treat in accordance with state law. All deviations shall be documented in the client record.

5.  Protocols shall not include prescription drugs. (Does not apply to protocols by APNs and RNPs.)

6.  The roles of the RN, LPN and LPTN are limited to the parameters set out in "Position Statement 95-1 Scopes of Practice." Because their practice parameters do not include assessment, the roles of the LPN and LPTN are limited to data collection in telenursing.

The "Position Statement 98-6 Decision Making Model" considers evolving practice potentials based on type of licensure and educational preparation. According to the model, "the licensed nurse is responsible and accountable, both professionally and legally for determining his/her personal scope of practice," within the boundaries set by the Nurse Practice Act and the ASBN Position Statements.

Nurses who practice telenursing may be requested to provide documentation that they have followed the "Position Statement 98-6 Decision Making Model" in making their decisions. The ASBN Positions Statements can be accessed at www.arsbn.org or at the Board office.

## 03-1 Application of School Nurse Guidelines in Patient Care Settings Other Than Schools
(undated)

It is the Board's opinion that the Arkansas State Board of Nursing School Nurse Roles and Responsibilities Practice Guidelines may be applied to settings other than schools provided they are used as a whole and not taken out of context. **Further it is the opinion of the Board that it is inappropriate to use these guidelines to approve or deny services to clients.**

In May 2000 the Arkansas State Board of Nursing approved practice guidelines for school nurses. These guidelines were developed to assist the school nurse in determining the nursing care activities that could safely be delegated when certain conditions were met. The guidelines may be applied to other similar
settings if:
1.  Nursing care is NOT the primary purpose of the client being in the setting,
2.  The parent/guardian would do the same nursing task(s) if they were present, and
3.  The parent/guardian has given their consent for the unlicensed person to perform the nursing tasks.

In addition, the nurse who delegates nursing care to an unlicensed person must apply the following criteria in determining if it is appropriate to delegate the care:

1. A licensed nurse responsible for the client's nursing care and qualified to determine the appropriate application of delegation to an unlicensed person must assess the client. Periodic reassessment must confirm that the nursing care being delegated to an unlicensed person continues to be appropriate.
2. The client's nursing care needs must be stable.
3. The performance of the nursing care by an unlicensed person must not pose a potential harm to the client.
4. No or little modification can be made in the nursing care provided the client.
5. The nursing care being provided for the client cannot involve ongoing assessments, interpretations, or decision-making.
6. The competency of the unlicensed person to perform the required nursing care is validated and documented. This requires the nurse who is delegating the nursing care to be familiar with the client's needs and with the unlicensed person's skills.
7. Supervision that is required for the individual unlicensed person performing the specific task(s) for a specific client is readily available.
8. The facilities' policies and procedures identify the task(s) that may be delegated to an unlicensed person. The policies and procedures must also recognize that the nurse who is delegating the task(s) is responsible for determining that a task is appropriate to delegate in a specific situation.

Nurses who delegate nursing tasks are responsible and accountable for ensuring that the delegation was appropriate. Unlicensed persons are responsible and accountable for competent performance of the nursing care that is delegated to them which includes calling the delegating nurse for assistance if the client's condition or needs change.

### 03-2 Assistive Personnel Applying and Measuring Tuberculin Skin Tests
Approved November 13, 2003

Assistive personnel may apply and measure tuberculin skin tests provided the following requirements are met.

1. The assistive personnel work under the supervision of a Registered Nurse employed by the Arkansas Department of Health.
2. The assistive personnel satisfactorily completes a course in applying and measuring tuberculin skin tests that includes:
   a. Five rights of medication administration
   b. Criteria for tuberculin testing
   c. Technique for administering antigen
   d. Measuring & documenting negative and reactive skin tests
   e. Criteria for immediate reporting of results to the nurse

f. Minimum of 20 observed applications and 20 observed test measurements & documentations.

3. The assistive personnel contact the RN for direction in determining if a tuberculin test is warranted when new contacts are identified.
4. The assistive personnel notify the RN of any reaction.
5. Competency is periodically re-evaluated and documented by the supervising RN.

—— **School Nurse Roles & Responsibilities**
May 2000, Revised September 2007

**Arkansas State Board of Nursing**
**School Nurse Roles & Responsibilities**
**Practice Guidelines**

**Developed in collaboration with the**
**Arkansas School Nurses Association**
**May 2000**
**Revised September 2007**

**Arkansas State Board of Nursing**
**School Nurse Roles and Responsibilities**
**Practice Guidelines**

**The School Nurse strengthens and facilitates the educational process by promoting and protecting the health of students and staff. School Nurses modify or remove health related barriers to learning, assess the health care needs, and link the health service program with education and support services (ASBN 1999).**

The Arkansas State Board of Nursing and Arkansas School Nurses Association collaborated to provide guidelines for nursing practice in the school setting. These guidelines will assist school nurses, educators, and administrators in determining the care and staff qualifications that are required for the health and welfare of their student population. While the school nurse and school environment are specifically named in the guidelines, the same principles are to be applied to any setting where nurses are acting in loco parentis:

**In loco parentis** / in lówkow pəréntəs/. In the place of a parent; instead of a parent; charged, factitiously, with a parent's rights, duties,

"Loco parentis" exists when person undertakes care and control of another in absence of such supervision by latter's natural parents and in absence of formal legal approval, and is temporary in character and is not to be likened to an adoption which is permanent (Black, 1990).

While the nurse is acting in place of the parent the nurse must obey all laws as defined in the *Arkansas Nurse Practice Act (NPA) and Arkansas State Board of Nursing.* In addition to the NPA, the nurse needs to be aware and follow any law that applies to his/her area of practice, such as but not limited to those that are under the jurisdiction of the Arkansas Department of Health and Arkansas Department of Education.

The following nurses have graciously given their time, energy and expertise in developing these guidelines:

2007 Revision Task Group

| | |
|---|---|
| Melanie Allen –Vilonia | Valerie Beshears – Fort Smith |
| Margo Bushmiaer – Little Rock | Sandra Campbell – North Little Rock |
| Lisa Drake – Forrest City | Lori Eakin – ASBN Board Member |
| Cassandra Harvey – ASBN Board Member | Kathey Haynie – Bryant |
| Sandra Kinsey – England | Paula Smith – State School Nurse Consultant |

## Table of Contents

---

### Arkansas State Board of Nursing
### School Nurse Roles and Responsibilities
### Practice Guidelines

Changes in American society, nursing practice and the nature of youth health services have resulted in an increased demand for expert clinical health services in youth oriented settings, such as schools, camps, day care centers and juvenile detention centers. Advances in health care and technology have increased the survival rate and life expectancy of low birth weight infants, children with chronic illnesses, congenital anomalies and those who have survived traumatic injuries. Some of these children have special healthcare needs, such as technology assistance, medication and treatment administration, and supplemental nutrition that must be addressed while the child is away from home. An even greater number of children have long-term chronic medical conditions such as diabetes, asthma, anemia, hemophilia, epilepsy, and leukemia. Some of these conditions require daily management in a setting outside of the home, while other conditions may require only intermittent management or acute care procedures on an emergency basis. These changes have also heightened the need for population based health promotion, prevention, and early intervention services in youth oriented settings. Safe and accountable nursing practice requires adherence to the nursing process (assessment, diagnosis, outcome identification, planning, implementation, and evaluation) and systematic, continuous documentation of the individual care provided to clients.

Two statutes from the Education Chapter of the Arkansas Code specifically address the issue of providing for a child's healthcare needs and who is to perform the tasks required.

A.C.A. § 6-18-1005(a)(6)(A) "Students with special health care needs, including the chronically ill, medically fragile, and technology-dependent and students with other health impairments shall have individualized health care plans."

178

A.C.A. §6-18-1005 (a)(6)(B)(i) "Invasive medical procedures required by students and provided at the school shall be performed by trained, licensed personnel who are licensed to perform the task subject to §17-87-102 (6)(D) or other professional licensure statutes."

The Nurse Practice Act that regulates the practice of nursing is referenced in the above statute.

**A.C.A. §17-87-102 (6)** "Practice of professional [registered] nursing" means the performance for compensation of any acts involving:
> (A) The observation, care, and counsel of the ill, injured, or infirm;
> (B) The maintenance of health or prevention of illness of others;
> (C) The supervision and teaching of other personnel;
> **(D) The delegation of certain nursing practices to other personnel as set forth in regulations established by the board; or**
> (E) The administration of medications and treatments as prescribed by practitioners authorized to prescribe and treat in accordance with state law where such acts require substantial specialized judgment and skill based on knowledge and application of the principles of biological, physical, and social sciences.

The ASBN interprets these statutes to require the school to provide for the development of an individualized healthcare plan (IHP) by personnel who are qualified through education and licensure to perform the task. Furthermore, the school is required to provide for the tasks identified in the IHP to be performed by personnel under the direction of a registered nurse (RN) in accordance with the Nurse Practice Act, ASBN Rules and Position Statements. The RN may delegate or assign specific tasks to be performed by a licensed practical nurse (LPN), licensed psychiatric technician nurse (LPTN), or unlicensed assistive personnel (UAP.) Scopes of practice of the RN, LPN, LPTN, and UAP are defined on pages [below].

In order to provide the necessary services, schools must clarify the roles, responsibilities and liabilities of the health care team; including various professionals and unlicensed assistive personnel as they work together to meet the health care needs of children. A health care team may include many different professionals, each licensed within the State of Arkansas. Licensure acts delineate the services that each professional may perform.

**School Nurse Role Description:**

School nursing practice is one of the most rapidly expanding subspecialties of nursing. Increased attention has focused on the schools as a site where prevention, early intervention, and primary care can occur. The school nursing role has changed to incorporate an increased responsibility for managing the health service program and has expanded clinical skills to serve students with a wide range of health risks, illnesses, and disabilities. The role, duty, responsibility, and employment of the School Nurse must comply with the *Arkansas Nurse Practice Act and Arkansas State Board of Nursing Rules*. The School Nurse is responsible for the development, implementation, evaluation and revision of the individualized health care plan for each student with special health care needs under his/her supervision. The School Nurse is responsible for practicing within their scope of practice.

The profession of nursing is a dynamic discipline. Practice potentials change and develop in response to health care needs of society, technical advancements, and the expansion of scientific knowledge. All licensed nurses share a common base of responsibility and accountability defined as the practice of nursing. However, competency based practice scopes of individual nurses may vary according to the type of basic licensure preparation, practice experiences, and professional development activities. The parameters of the practice are defined by basic licensure preparation and advanced education. Within the scope of practice, all nurses should remain current and increase their expertise and skill in a variety of ways, e.g., practice experience, in-service education, and continuing education. Practice responsibility, and relative levels of independence are also expanded in this way. The licensed nurse is responsible and accountable, both professionally and legally, for determining his/her personal scope of nursing practice. Since the roles and responsibilities of nurses, and consequently the scope of nursing practice, is ever changing and increasing in complexity, it is important that the nurse makes decisions regarding his/her own scope of practice (ASBN 1998.)

**Scope of Practice:**

The following are excerpts from the Arkansas Nurse Practice Act and Arkansas State Board of Nursing Rules that define nursing and the scope of practice based on educational preparation and experience.

**The Practice of Professional (Registered) Nursing:**

*The delivery of health care services which require **assessment, diagnosis, planning, intervention, and evaluation** fall within the professional nurse scope of practice.* (ASBN, 1995.) **ACA § 17-87-102 (6)** The performance for compensation of any acts involving:

(A)  The observation, care and counsel of the ill, injured or infirm;
(B)  The maintenance of health or prevention of illness of others;
(C)  The supervision and teaching of other personnel;
(D)  The delegation of certain nursing practices to other personnel as set forth in regulations established by the board;
(E)  Administration of medications and treatments as prescribed by practitioners authorized to prescribe and treat in accordance with state law where such acts require substantial specialized judgment and skill based on knowledge and application of the principles of

biological, physical and social sciences.

**The Practice of Advanced Practice Nursing:**

*The advanced practice nurse shall practice in accordance with the scope of practice defined by the appropriate national certifying body and the standards set forth in the ASBN Rules. The advanced practice nurse may provide health care for which the APN is educationally prepared and for which competence has been attained and maintained.* (ASBN,1995.)

**ACA § 17-87-102(4)** The delivery of health care services for compensation by professional nurses who have gained additional knowledge and skills through successful completion of an organized program of nursing education that certifies nurses for advanced practice roles as advanced nurse practitioners, certified nurse anesthetists, certified nurse midwives, and clinical nurse specialists.

**The Practice of Registered Nurse Practitioner Nursing:**

**ACA § 17-87-102(8)(A)** The delivery of health care services for compensation in collaboration with and under the direction of a licensed physician or under the direction of protocols developed with a licensed physician.

**The Practice of Practical Nursing:**
The delivery of health care services which are performed under the direction of the professional nurse, licensed physician, or licensed dentist, including **observation, intervention, and evaluation,** fall within the LPN/LPTN scope of practice (ASBN,1995.)

**ACA § 17-87-102 (5)** The performance for compensation of acts involving:
   • the care of the ill, injured, or infirm;
   • the delegation of certain nursing practices to other personnel under the direction of a registered professional nurse, an advanced practice nurse, a licensed physician or a licensed dentist, which acts do not require the substantial specialized skill, judgment, and knowledge required in professional nursing.

**The Practice of Psychiatric Technician Nursing:**
*The delivery of health care services which are performed under the direction of the professional nurse, licensed physician, or licensed dentist, including observation, intervention, and evaluation, fall within the LPN/LPTN scope of practice* (ASBN,1995.)

**ACA § 17-87-102(7)** The performance for compensation of acts involving:
• the care of the physically and mentally ill, retarded, injured, or infirm;
• the delegation of certain nursing practices to other personnel

181

• the carrying out of medical orders under the direction of a registered professional nurse, an advanced practice nurse, a licensed physician or a licensed dentist, where such activities do not require the substantial specialized skill, judgment, and knowledge required in professional nursing.

## Unlicensed Assistive Personnel

Definitions of the RN, LPN, and LPTN allow each to delegate certain nursing practices to other personnel such as unlicensed assistive personnel.

### Registered Nurses
### ACA § 17-87-102(6)
(C) The supervision and teaching of other personnel;
(D) The delegation of certain nursing practices to other personnel as set forth in regulations established by the board;

### Licensed Practical Nurses
### ACA § 17-87-102(5):
• the delegation of certain nursing practices to other personnel

### Licensed Psychiatric Technician Nurses
### ACA § 17-87-102(7)
• the delegation of certain nursing practices to other personnel

The scope of practice of the Unlicensed Assistive Personnel (UAP) is further defined in the Arkansas State Board of Nursing Rules, Chapter 5 on Delegation. (ASBN, 2007.)

**Note: Regardless of the school districts titling of the position or other job duties, when individuals are providing services listed in the Nursing Task List (pages [below]) or other similar services, the delegation and supervision rules apply. Individuals who violate the Nurse Practice Act by practicing nursing without a license are subject to civil and/or administrative prosecution as allowed in A.C.A. §17-87-104.**

## School Nurse Role Description

The school nurse is required to fulfill many functions within the school setting. The following role descriptions are adapted from School Nursing: A Comprehensive Text (Wolfe, 2006).

1. **Clinician:** 1) The Registered Nurse is a skilled clinician providing daily nursing care and case management during school hours. Assessing, making effective nursing diagnoses, choosing appropriate interventions, and identifying outcomes are essential skills all school nurses must possess. School nurses develop individual health plans, administer medications and treatments and monitor for compliance or attainment of expected outcomes. 2) Under the direction of an

RN, APN, licensed physician or licensed dentist the Licensed Practical Nurse implements the individual health plan, administers medications and treatments and monitors the student or staff for compliance or meeting expected outcomes.

2. **Advocate:** Providing a physically and emotionally safe environment is the primary goal in meeting the needs of the students and staff. This is accomplished through advocacy and negotiating skills. The nurse may also advocate for system changes to meet the health needs of the students and staff.

3. **Collaborator:** School nurses help families navigate complex medical systems and identify resources for healthcare services, financial resources, shelter, food and health promotion.

4. **Health Educator:** The school nurse collaborates with administrators and teachers in providing health education opportunities and experiences for school age children, families, school personnel and the community that will lead to health behavior change.

5. **Liaison:** As the health liaison to the community, the school nurse is a translator of educational and medical goals and a coordinator between the school and medical communities. It is necessary for the school nurse to possess the ability to communicate effectively with practitioners from education and healthcare while taking every opportunity to promote and clarify the role of the school nurse as an influential and effective partner.

## Standards of School Nursing Practice
## And Professional Performance

The Standards of School Nursing Practice and their accompanying measurement criteria describe and measure a competent level of school nursing practice and professional performance. Built on American Nurses Association's *Nursing: Scope and Standards of Practice* (ANA, 2004) for registered nurses, these standards are authoritative statements of the accountability, direction, and evaluation of individuals in this special nursing practice. Composed of two sets – the Standards of Practice and the Standards of Professional Performance – these standards define how outcomes for school nurse activities can be measured.

The Standards of Practice reflect the six steps of the nursing process (assessment, diagnosis, outcomes identification, implementation, planning and evaluation), which is the foundation for the critical thinking of all registered nurses. The Standards of Professional Performance describe the behaviors expected of the nurse in the role of a school nurse. (ANA, 2005)

# Standards of Practice

**Standard 1. Assessment**

The school nurse collects comprehensive data pertinent to the client's health or the situation.

**Standard 2. Diagnosis**

The school nurse analyzes the assessment data to determine the diagnosis or issues.

**Standard 3. Outcomes Identification**

The school nurse identifies expected outcomes for a plan individualized to the client or the situation.

**Standard 4. Planning**

The school nurse develops a plan that prescribes strategies and alternatives to attain expected outcomes.

**Standard 5. Implementation**

The school nurse implements the identified plan.

**Standard 5A: Coordination of Care**

The school nurse coordinates care delivery.

**Standard 5B: Health Teaching and Health Promotion**

The school nurse provides health education and employs strategies to promote health and a safe environment.

**Standard 5C: Consultation**

The school nurse provides consultation to influence the identified plan, enhance the abilities of others, and effect change.

**Standard 5D: Prescriptive Authority and Treatment**

The advanced practice registered nurse uses prescriptive authority, procedures, referrals, treatments, and therapies in accordance with state and federal laws and regulations.

**Standard 6. Evaluation**

The school nurse evaluates progress towards achievement of outcomes.

# Standards of Professional Performance

## Standard 7.  Quality of Practice
The school nurse systematically enhances the quality and effectiveness of nursing practice.

## Standard 8.  Education
The school nurse attains knowledge and competency that reflects current school nursing practice.

## Standard 9.  Professional Practice Evaluation
The school nurse evaluates one's own nursing practice in relation to professional standards and guidelines, relevant statues, rules and regulations.

## Standard 10.  Collegiality
The school nurse interacts with, and contributes to the professional development, of peers school personnel as colleagues.

## Standard 11.  Collaboration
The school nurse collaborates with the client, the family, school staff, and others in the conduct of school nursing practice.

## Standard 12.  Ethics
The school nurse integrates ethical provisions in all areas of practice.

## Standard 13.  Research
The school nurse integrates research findings into practice.

## Standard 14.  Resource Utilization
The school nurse considers factors related to safety, effectiveness, cost, and impact on practice in the planning and delivery of school nursing services.

## Standard 15.  Leadership
The school nurse provides leadership in the professional practice setting and the profession.

## Standard 16.  Program Management
The school nurse manages school health services.

## School Nurses Qualifications

The *Arkansas Nurse Practice Act* (NPA) and ASBN Scopes of Practice Position Statement authorize the professional nurse (RN) to provide nursing care. Licensed practical nurses (LPN) and licensed psychiatric technician nurses (LPTN) provide nursing care under the direction of an RN, APN, licensed physician or dentist.

The Education Chapter of the Arkansas Code addresses the issue of providing for a child's healthcare needs and who is to perform the tasks required.

> A.C.A. § 6-18-1005(a)(6)(A) "Students with special health care needs, including the chronically ill, medically fragile, and technology-dependent and students with other health impairments shall have individualized health care plans."

> A.C.A. § 6-18-1005 (a)(6)(B)(i) "Invasive medical procedures required by students and provided at the school shall be performed by trained, licensed personnel who are licensed to perform the task subject to **§ 17-87-102(6)(D)** or other professional licensure statutes."

The Arkansas Department of Education Resource Guide: Developing School Policies on Children with Special Health Care Needs (2007) requires the school district to:

> "ensure that appropriate training is provided for all school district personnel. The school district must address the issue of using only qualified, trained personnel to provide health care procedures and services. Policies should indicate that personnel performing health care services must be appropriately trained, credentialed and/or licensed prior to administering health care services. The school district should address continuing education for licensure of the nurse as part of its Comprehensive System of Personnel Development (CSPD) plan. This continuing education will ensure the nurse's competency in providing quality care for the students of the school district.

It is recommended that the school nurse hold the following minimum qualifications:

A. **Nurse Supervisor** – Coordinates and supervises nursing activities of one or more licensed nurses in one or more school districts.
   1. Hold an active Professional Nursing License (RN)
   2. 5 years licensed nursing experience (2 of which must have been as an RN)
   3. 3 years experience as a school nurse
   4. 1 year experience as a supervisor (preferred)
   5. Current certification in Cardiopulmonary Resuscitation for healthcare providers with AED and First Aid

6. Current certification in Scoliosis, Hearing, Vision and Growth (height and weight) screening

B. **Registered Nurse/Registered Nurse Practitioner**
1. Hold an active Professional Nursing License (RN)
2. 2 years licensed nursing experience (3 years preferred)
3. Current certification in Cardiopulmonary Resuscitation for healthcare providers with AED and First Aid
4. Current certification in Scoliosis, Hearing, Vision and Growth (height and weight) screening

C. **Licensed Practical Nurse/Licensed Psychiatric Technician Nurse**
1. Hold an active LPN/LPTN Nursing License
2. 2 years licensed nursing experience (3 years preferred)
3. Current certification in Cardiopulmonary Resuscitation for healthcare providers with AED and First Aid
4. Current certification in Scoliosis, Hearing, Vision and Growth (height and weight) screening

D. **Advanced Practice Nurse**
1. Hold an active Advanced Practice Nurse License
2. Certification in a field that includes pediatrics
3. 2 years APN experience
4. Current certification in Cardiopulmonary Resuscitation for healthcare providers with AED and First Aid
5. Current certification in Scoliosis, Hearing, Vision and Growth (height and weight) screening

## Unlicensed Assistive Personnel (UAP) Qualifications

Unlicensed Assistive Personnel are those individuals who provide any of the nursing tasks listed in the Nursing Task List on pages [below] any similar nursing care task.

It is recommended that the Unlicensed Assistive Personnel who provide nursing care to students hold the following minimum qualifications prior to providing care:

1. Have a high school diploma or the equivalent;
2. Have successfully completed a literacy and reading comprehension screening process;
3. Have current certification in Cardiopulmonary Resuscitation and First Aid as provided by the American Red Cross or American Heart Association.
4. Have successfully completed training and competency validation in performing

nursing tasks that are to be delegated by a nurse.

**Note: Regardless of the school districts titling of the position or other job duties, when individuals are providing services listed in the Nursing Task List (pages xxx-xxx) or other similar services, the delegation and supervision rules apply. Individuals who violate the Nurse Practice Act by practicing nursing without a license are subject to civil and/or administrative prosecution as allowed in A.C.A. § 17-87-104.**

## Supervision

Only the school nurse can determine medically necessary nursing care that can be safely delegated to unlicensed assistive personnel and under what circumstances. Sometimes confusion exists when an unlicensed assistive person is asked to do a procedure that a parent has been doing at home. For example, some parents have been taught to give intravenous medication. The assumption is made that because a parent has been administering the medication intravenously, any school employee can do it. Family members can legally provide nursing care without a nursing license as an allowable exception to the Nurse Practice Act. However, when these services are transferred to the public, the *Nurse Practice Act* applies. **While administrators, teachers, and parents may be helpful resources and allies, they may not have the knowledge base to make adequate judgments about delegation of medical or nursing care; nor can they be held legally accountable to the same extent that a nurse will be liable for nursing care delivered. The school nurse may be accountable to the administrator for personnel issues but the nurse is responsible for directing nursing care.**

## Supervision Defined

Merriam-Webster On-Line Dictionary defines supervision as "a critical watching and directing (as of activities or a course of action.)" The American Nurses Association defines supervision as "the active process of directing, guiding, and influencing the outcome of an individual's performance of an activity." Supervision does not require the supervisor to physically be present 100% of the time, however, the supervisor must be able to critically watch and direct the Licensed Practical Nurse's (LPN's) and/or Unlicensed Assistive Person's (UAP's) activities or course of action. The amount of supervision required is directly related to the individual LPN's or UAP's experience, skills and abilities and the healthcare needs of the students being served.

## School Nurses:

School nurses though supervised administratively by a superintendent or principal, are responsible for health services and nursing care administered through the health services program. Schools may utilize a team consisting of RN(s), LPN(s), LPTN(s) and/or Unlicensed Assistive Personnel (UAPs) to provide health services. In accordance with the NPA and ASBN Scope of Practice Position Statement, RNs assess, diagnose, plan, implement and evaluate nursing care. The LPN/LPTN under the direction of an RN, APN, licensed physician or dentist observes, implements, and evaluates nursing care. Healthcare unlicensed assistive personnel (UAPs) perform delegated nursing care in accordance with the ASBN Rules.

## Registered Nurse

The Nurse Practice Act defines Professional or Registered Nursing as follows:
**ACA § 17-87-102(6)** The performance for compensation of any acts involving:
(A) The observation, care and counsel of the ill, injured or infirm;
(B) The maintenance of health or prevention of illness of others;
(C) The supervision and teaching of other personnel;
(D) The delegation of certain nursing practices to other personnel as set forth in regulations established by the board;
(E) Administration of medications and treatments as prescribed by practitioners authorized to prescribe and treat in accordance with state law where such acts require substantialspecialized judgment and skill based on knowledge and application of the principles of biological, physical and social sciences.

While the Registered Nurse has autonomy in providing nursing care she/he must have a prescription from a practitioner authorized to prescribe and treat in order to administer medications and/or treatments that require substantial specialized judgment and skill based on knowledge and application of the principles of biological, physical and social science.

## Licensed Practice Nurses/Licensed Psychiatric Technician Nurses

The *Nurse Practice Act* requires the Licensed Practical Nurse (LPN) and Licensed Psychiatric Technician Nurse (LPTN) to work under the direction of a Registered Nurse (RN,) Practice Nurse (APN,) physician or dentist:

**A.C.A. § 17-87-102(5)** Practice of practical nursing means the performance for compensation of acts involving the care of the ill, injured, or infirm or the delegation of certain nursing practices to other personnel as set forth in regulations established by the board under the direction of a registered professional nurse, an advanced practice nurse, a licensed physician, or a licensed dentist, which acts do not require the substantial specialized skill, judgment and knowledge required in professional nursing.

189

The Arkansas State Board of Nursing *Position Statement 98-6 Scope of Practice Decision Making Model* defines the LPN/LPTN scope of practice as:

"The delivery of healthcare services which are performed under the direction of the professional nurse, licensed physician or licensed dentist, including observation, interventions, and evaluation, fall within the LPN/LPTN scope of practice"

The Arkansas State Board of Nursing *Position Statement 98-6 Scope of Practice Decision Making Model* defines the RN scope of practice as:

"The delivery of healthcare services which require assessment, diagnosis, planning, intervention, and evaluation fall within the professional nurse scope of practice."

Based on these references, under the direction of an RN, APN, physician, or dentist the LPN may provide healthcare services that do **not** require assessment, diagnosis or planning.

Statutes in the Education Chapter of the Arkansas Code require the school to provide individual healthcare plans (IHP) for students with healthcare needs. The statute also requires those who are providing the care in the IHP to be trained and licensed in accordance with the appropriate professional licensing statutes and rules. The IHP inherently requires assessment, diagnosis and planning. The RN and APN have these skills within their professional scope of practice.

A chart within these guidelines identifies nursing procedures that students could require while attending school. Included in the chart is identification of those who are qualified to perform the task with supervision and inservice education. Nursing procedures that specifically require the LPN to be supervised include:

- Naso-gastric (N/G) Feeding and Monitoring
- Gastrostomy Feeding and Monitoring
- Jejunostomy Tube Feeding
- Total Parenteral Feeding (intravenous) and Monitoring
- Clean Intermittent and Sterile Catheterization
- Ventricular Peritoneal Shunt Monitoring
- Mechanical Ventilator Monitoring
- Mechanical Ventilator Ambubag
- Intermittent and Continuous Oxygen
- Central Line Catheter management
- Peritoneal Dialysis
- Medication Administration by all routes
- Ostomy Care and Irrigation
- Pharyngeal and Tracheostomy Suctioning

- Screening, growth, vital signs, vision, hearing, scoliosis
- Blood and Urine Glucose testing
- Seizure Procedures
- Pressure Ulcer Care
- Sterile and Non-sterile Dressings

This document also identifies nursing procedures that the LPN is not qualified to perform. The following are included:

- Nutritional Assessment
- Gastrostomy Tube Reinsertion
- Adjustment of Ventilator
- Developing Protocols such as
     - Healthcare Procedures,
     - Emergency Protocols, and
     - Individualized Healthcare Plans.


## Unlicensed Assistive Personnel:

**School unlicensed assistive personnel/education assistants may be assigned to a particular school building and are accountable to the principal for personnel and school building functions; however, they must have licensed nursing supervision when they are delegated nursing tasks.** Special education assistants are accountable to the special education director for personnel and activities related to the student's special education plan. Given the complexity of answering to two supervising authorities, the role of the school health unlicensed assistive personnel/special education assistant warrants continuous support.


## Private Duty Care:

As the school and school nurse are responsible for ensuring safe nursing care is provided when the student is under their care, the school is encouraged to develop policies requiring private duty nurses and private duty unlicensed assistive persons to report to the school nurse. The plan of care/action is to be reviewed. The private duty nurse or UAP is responsible for following the school's policies and procedures regarding health care. The private duty health care provider is accountable to deliver care within their scope of practice parameters and the Nurse Practice Act.

## Complaints to the Arkansas State Board of Nursing

If the Board of Nursing receives a complaint regarding a nurse's practice in a school, the Board's Staff will conduct an investigation. The nurse may be asked to provide evidence that the nursing procedures they perform are within their personal scope of practice. If it is determined that the nurse has violated the Nurse Practice Act disciplinary action may be taken.

When a complaint is filed regarding an LPN/LPTN, the Board may ask the LPN to show evidence that they work under the direction of an RN, APN, or physician. Evidence may include but would not be limited to:
- job description,
- documentation of competency validation,
- policies and procedures
- attendance records of continuing education provided by the supervising / directing RN, APN, physician, or dentist or
- a statement from the RN, APN, physician, or dentist who evaluates the nursing care provided by the LPN regarding compliance with policies and procedures set up by the RN, APN, or physician.

## Disciplinary Action

Any nurse who violates the Nurse Practice Act is subject to disciplinary action by the Arkansas State Board of Nursing. Disciplinary action against the license could include any of the following:
- Letter of Reprimand
- Board Reprimand
- Probation
- Suspension
- Revocation

## Disciplinary Action of Unlicensed Assistive Personnel

Individuals who violate the Nurse Practice Act by practicing nursing without a license are subject to civil and/or administrative prosecution as allowed in A.C.A. § 17-87-104.

### § 17-87-104. Penalty
(a)(1) It shall be a misdemeanor for any person to: ...
(C) Practice professional nursing, advanced practice nursing, registered nurse practitioner nursing, practical nursing, or psychiatric technician nursing as defined by this chapter unless licensed by the Arkansas State Board of Nursing to do so;
(2) Such misdemeanor shall be punishable by a fine of not less than twenty-five dollars ($25.00) nor more than five hundred dollars ($500). Each subsequent

offense shall be punishable by fine or by imprisonment of not more than thirty (30) days, or by both fine and imprisonment.

(b)(1) After providing notice and a hearing, the board may levy civil penalties in an amount not to exceed one thousand dollars ($1000) for each violation against those individuals or entities found to be in violation of this chapter or regulations promulgated thereunder.

(2) Each day of violation shall be a separate offense

## Principles of Delegation

**The decision to delegate nursing care rests with the judgment of RN, LPN, LPTN, or APN. Only a licensed nurse may determine that a UAP or other school staff can safely deliver the care.**

Factors to consider when delegating nursing care include:

1. The **complexity** of the child's condition and the nursing care that is required: A routine dressing change is less likely to result in complications than the administration of IV medications, even if both are done poorly. Consider the question: What are the risks to the student if this procedure is done improperly?

2. The **dynamics** of the child's status or frequency with which nursing care requirements change: A newly inserted tracheostomy presents significantly different problems than one that has been in place for ten years. A student with Type I diabetes who has many insulin reactions and a noon glucometer check with directions for varying the insulin dosage is different than a student who is stable with a noon glucometer check to validate stable blood sugar levels.

3. The **knowledge and skills** that are required to complete the task: Feeding through a nasal gastric feeding tube requires knowledge and skills that are not required in a gastrostomy tube feeding.

4. The **technology** that is employed in providing the nursing care; Assess whether the unlicensed assistive personnel has had appropriate training to perform the task or operate equipment required in performing the task that is being delegated. Using a glucometer to monitor a stable client's blood sugar requires less knowledge and skill than adjusting the settings a ventilator.

5. The amount of **supervision** that is required by the unlicensed assistive personnel to whom the task is being delegated: Has the unlicensed assistive personnel demonstrated the ability to competently perform the task and is that competency documented in their

personnel file? Since the competency was documented, has the individual performed the task frequently enough to maintain competency?

6.      The **availability** of the licensed nurse for supervision: Is a written plan of care and up-to-date policy and procedure manual readily accessible to the unlicensed assistive personnel? Does the unlicensed assistive personnel know the signs and symptoms that require them to call for assistance and/or to report to the licensed nurse? Is the licensed nurse who delegated the task readily available in person or telephonic communications?

7.      Relevant **safety and infection control** issues: Has the unlicensed assistive personnel had the training and competency validation to safely perform the task and utilize infection control principles.

8.      **Healthcare Policies and Procedures:** School nurses are responsible for ensuring current policies and procedures are available to guide the nursing care that is delivered. While District School Boards may review and approve internal policies and procedures, the school nurse is accountable for maintaining current nursing practice standards.

In accordance with the *Arkansas State Board of Nursing Rules and Regulations* Chapter Five on Delegation policies and procedures are to:

**Recognize nursing tasks that can be delegated without prior assessment including:**
a.      Activities of Daily Living
b.      Noninvasive and non-sterile treatments
c.      Data collection
d.      Ambulating, positioning, turning
e.      Personal hygiene
f.      Oral feeding
g.      Socialization activities

**Recognize nursing tasks that SHALL NOT be delegated:**
a.      Physical, psychological, and social assessment which requires nursing judgment, intervention, referral or follow-up
b.      Formulation of the plan of nursing care and evaluation of the client's response to care rendered
c.      Specific tasks which require nursing judgment or intervention
d.      The responsibility and accountability for student health teaching and health counseling which promotes student education and involves the student's significant others in accomplishing health goals.
e.      Administration of intravenous medications or fluids.
f.      Receiving or transmitting verbal or telephone orders

**Recognize specific nursing tasks that MAY be delegated provided the five rights of delegation are followed:**
a.     Right Task
b.     Right Person
c.     Right Circumstances
d.     Right Communication
e.     Right Supervision

**Recognize that the nurse is responsible for determining that a task is appropriate to delegate in a specific situation.**

## Delegation of Specific Tasks

The following table is to be used to determine to whom specific tasks may be delegated.

Only the Nurse responsible for the student's nursing care may determine which nursing tasks may be delegated to an Unlicensed Assistive Person. The tasks listed in the chart below may only be delegated if the Five Rights of Delegation are met. Refer to the section on Delegation Principles.

**After assessment and consideration of the principles of delegation, the decision to delegate nursing care must be based on the following:**
1. Child's nursing care needs are stable.
2. Performance of the task does not pose a potential harm to the child.
3. Task involves little or no modification.
4. Task has a predictable outcome.
5. Task does not inherently involve ongoing assessments, interpretations or decision making.
6. The unlicensed assistive personnel's skills and competency levels.
7. The availability of supervision.

| | | | | | NURSING TASKS | | | |
|---|---|---|---|---|---|---|---|---|

<table>
<tr><td colspan="2">A = Within Scope of Practice<br>S = Within Scope of Practice with supervision<br>D = Delegated task with supervision<br>EM = In emergencies<br>X = Cannot perform</td><td colspan="3">Provider = Person w/legal authority to prescribe – M.D., APN with prescriptive authority, Dentist, Physician Assistant with prescriptive authority, etc.</td></tr>
</table>

| Procedure | Provider Order Required | RN | LPN/LPN | Unlicensed Assistive Personnel | Self | RN Scope of Practice: The delivery of health care services which require assessment, diagnosis, planning, intervention, and evaluation.  LPN Scope of Practice: The delivery of health care services which are performed under the direction of the professional nurse, licensed physician, or licensed dentist, including observation, intervention and evaluation | | |
|---|---|---|---|---|---|---|---|---|
| **1.0 Activities of Daily Living** | | | | | | | | |
| 1.1 Toileting/Diapering | | A | A | A | | | | |
| 1.2 Bowel/Bladder Training | | A | A | D | S | | | |
| 1.3 Dental Hygiene | | A | A | S | S | | | |
| 1.4 Oral Hygiene | | A | A | S | S | | | |
| 1.5 Lifting/Positioning Transfers | | A | A | S | S | | | |
| 1.6 Feeding | | | | | | | | |
| 1.6.1 Nutritional Assessment | | A | X | X | X | | | |
| 1.6.2 Oral Feeding | | A | A | S | A | | | |
| 1.6.3 Naso-Gastric Feeding | Yes | A | S | X | S | | | |
| 1.6.4 Monitoring N/G Feeding | | A | S | X | S | | | |
| 1.6.5 Gastrostomy Feeding | Yes | A | S | D | S | | | |
| 1.6.6 Monitoring Gastrostomy Feeding | | A | S | D | S | | | |
| 1.6.7 Jejunostomy Tube Feeding | Yes | A | S | X | X | | | |
| 1.6.8 Total Parenteral Feeding (intravenous) | Yes | A | S | X | X | | | |
| 1.6.9 Monitoring Parenteral Feeding | | A | S | X | X | | | |
| 1.6.10 Naso-Gastric Tube Feeding | Yes | A | S | X | X | | | |
| 1.6.11 Naso-Gastric Tube Removal | Yes | A | S | EM | S | | | |
| 1.6.12 Gastrostomy Tube Reinsertion | Yes | X | X | X | X | | | |
| **2.0 Urinary Catheterization** | | | | | | | | |

| | | |
|---|---|---|
| A = Within Scope of Practice<br>S = Within Scope of Practice with supervision<br>D = Delegated task with supervision<br>EM = In emergencies<br>X = Cannot perform | | Provider = Person w/legal authority to prescribe – M.D., APN with prescriptive authority, Dentist, Physician Assistant with prescriptive authority, etc. |

| Procedure | Provider Order Required | RN | LPN/LPTN | Unlicensed Assistive Personnel | Self | RN Scope of Practice: The delivery of health care services which require assessment, diagnosis, planning, intervention, and evaluation.<br><br>LPN Scope of Practice: The delivery of health care services which are performed under the direction of the professional nurse, licensed physician, or licensed dentist, including observation, intervention and evaluation. |
|---|---|---|---|---|---|---|
| 2.1 Clean Intermittent Cath. | Yes | A | S | D | S | |
| 2.2 Sterile Catheterization | Yes | A | S | X | X | |
| 2.3 External Catheter application | Yes | A | A | S | S | |
| 2.4 Indwelling Catheter Care (cleanse with soap & water, empty bag) | | A | A | S | S | |
| **3.0 Medical Support Systems** | | | | | | |
| 3.1 Ventricular Peritoneal Shunt Monitoring | Yes | A | S | D | X | |
| 3.2 Mechanical Ventilator | | | | | | |
|    3.2.1 Monitoring | Yes | A | S | D | X | |
|    3.2.2 Adjustment of Ventilator | Yes | A | S | X | X | |
|    3.2.3 Ambubag | | A | S | EM | X | |
| 3.3 Oxygen | | | | | | |
|    3.3.1 Intermittent | Yes | A | S | D | X | |
|    3.3.1 Continuous – monitoring | Yes | A | S | D | S | |
| 3.4 Central Line Catheter | Yes | A | S | X | X | |
| 3.5 Peritoneal Dialysis | Yes | A | S | X | X | |
| **4.0 Medication administration** | | | | | | |
| 4.1 Oral – Prescription | Yes | A | S | D | X | |
| 4.2 Oral – Over the Counter (written parental consent) | | A | S | D | S | |
| 4.3 Injection | Yes | A | S | X | S | |
| 4.4 Epi-Pen Allergy Kit | Yes | A | S | EM/S | S | |
| 4.5 Inhalation | | | | | | |
|    4.51 Prophylactic/Routine asthma inhaler | Yes | A | S | D | S | |
|    4.52 Emergency/Rescue asthma inhaler | Yes | A | S | D | S | |
|    4.53 Nasal Insulin | Yes | A | S | X | X | |
|    4.54 Nasal controlled substance ( such as but not limited to Versed) | Yes | A | S | X | X | |
| 4.6 Rectal | Yes | A | S | X | X | |
| 4.7 Bladder Instillation | Yes | A | S | X | X | |
| 4.8 Eye/Ear Drops | Yes | A | S | D | X | |
| 4.9 Topical | Yes | A | S | D | X | |
| 4.10 Per Naso-gastric Tube | Yes | A | S | X | X | |
| 4.11 Per Gastrostomy Tube | Yes | A | S | D | X | |
| 4.12 Intravenous | Yes | A | S | X | X | |
| **5.0 Ostomies (colostomy, ileostomy)** | | | | | | |
| 5.1 Ostomy Care (empty bag, cleanse w soap & water) | | A | S | S | S | |
| 5.2 Ostomy Irrigation | Yes | A | S | X | S | |
| **6.0 Respiratory** | | | | | | |
| 6.1 Postural Drainage | Yes | A | S | D | X | |

## NURSING TASKS

| | | |
|---|---|---|
| \ = Within Scope of Practice | | |
| S = Within Scope of Practice with supervision | Provider = Person w/legal authority to prescribe – M.D., APN with prescriptive authority, Dentist, Physician Assistant with prescriptive authority, etc. | |
| D = Delegated task with supervision | | |
| EM = In emergencies | | |
| X = Cannot perform | | |

| Procedure | Provider Order Required | RN | LPN / LPN | Unlicensed Assistive Personnel | Self | RN Scope of Practice: The delivery of health care services which require assessment, diagnosis, planning, intervention, and evaluation. LPN Scope of Practice: The delivery of health care services which are performed under the direction of the professional nurse, licensed physician, or licensed dentist, including observation, intervention and evaluation |
|---|---|---|---|---|---|---|
| 6.2 Percussion | Yes | A | S | D | X | |
| 6.3 Suctioning | | | | | | |
|     6.3.1 Pharyngeal | Yes | A | S | D | X | |
|     6.3.2 Tracheostomy | Yes | A | S | D | X | |
| 6.4 Tracheostomy Tube Replacement | Yes | A | EM | EM | EM | |
| 6.5 Tracheostomy Care (clean/dress) | Yes | A | S | D | X | |
| **7.0 Screenings** | | | | | | |
|     7.1 Growth (height/weight) | | A | S | D | S | |
|     7.2 Vital Signs | | A | A | S | X | |
|     7.3 Hearing | | A | S | D | X | |
|     7.4 Vision | | A | S | X | X | |
|     7.5 Scoliosis | | A | S | D | X | |
| **8.0 Specimen Collecting/Testing** | | | | | | |
|     8.1 Blood Glucose | Yes | A | S | D | S | |
|     8.2 Urine Glucose Ketone | Yes | A | S | D | S | |
| **9.0 Other Healthcare Procedures** | | | | | | |
|     9.1 Seizure Safety Procedures | | A | S | D | X | |
|     9.2 Pressure Ulcer Care | Yes | A | S | D | X | |
|     9.3 Dressings, Sterile | | A | S | D | X | |
|     9.4 Dressings, Non-sterile | | A | S | D | S | |
|     9.5 Vagal Nerve Stimulator | Yes | A | S | D | X | |
| **10.0 Developing Protocols** | | | | | | |
|     10.1 Healthcare Procedures | | A | X | X | X | |
|     10.2 Emergency Protocols | | A | X | X | X | |
|     10.3 Individualized Healthcare Plan | | A | X | X | X | |

198

# Medication Administration

The Delegation Chapter of the Arkansas State Board of Nursing Rules and Regulations lists medication administration as a task that shall not be delegated to unlicensed persons. It is recognized that in the school, camp, day care center and juvenile detention center settings, the patient/client condition is generally stable, on routine or occasional as needed medications and the parent would medicate them in the same manner, if the parent were present. The licensed school nurse is responsible for the administration of medications. During times when the school nurse is not present, the administration of medications may be delegated to persons identified in the table for delegating specific tasks. A provider order and/or written permission from the parent/guardian must be on file for all medications administered "in loco parentis," in the place of the parent.

**The licensed nurse is responsible for identifying qualified persons to be trained to administer medications in the nurse's absence.** After training and documentation of the unlicensed person's competency, administering medications may be delegated as indicated in the nursing task chart and following the Principle's of Delegation and the Five Rights of Delegation

Each facility (school, camp, day care center, juvenile detentioncenter, etc.) shall have a written policy regarding the administration of medication. The policy should include at least the following:

- A provider order is required for all prescription medications. A label on a prescription bottle may serve as the prescription, if acceptable to the facility.
- Written parental permission is on file for all over the counter medications that are to be taken by the minor. Permission slips may be time limited, such as, the school year, a semester, one month, or one week, depending on the governing body policy.
- All medications must be in the original container.
- The container must specify special storage instructions if appropriate (insulin needs to be refrigerated.)
- Prescription medications are to be labeled with the student's legal name (on record with the facility), date Rx was filled, ordering provider name, name of medication, dose, route, and frequency.
- All medications will be given according to labeling directions on the container. Deviations from label directions will require a written provider order.
- Procedure for administering and documenting medications during field trips and extra curricular activities.
- Documentation methods for the receipt of medication and the administration of medication.
- Methods by which nurse will receive medication e.g., students may bring medication in with written authorization from parent/guardian or parent is required to deliver medication to the school nurse.

- Storage and security of medications.
- Access to medications in the absence of the school nurse.
- Accountability methods for controlled substances.
- Arkansas Department of Health – Pharmacy Services Rules requires controlled substances be kept under double locks.
- Nurses must establish a counting system to document the number of doses of a controlled substance brought to the school, such as counting the number of doses at the time they are delivered by the parent or student in the presence of the parent or student. Both must document the number delivered to the school. A count should be done periodically to verify the medication can be accounted for by documentation and the number on hand for the specific student. Access to controlled substances is to be limited to as few personnel as possible. When possible the licensed nurse is to access and administer controlled substances.

In addition the policy may specify the following:

- A requirement that the initial dose of a new medication must be given by the parent/guardian outside of the facility setting. A specific length of time may be required between the initial dose being given and the student's re-admittance to the facility.
- Reports to parents/guardians regarding medication administration.
- Parents/guardians are encouraged to administer medication at home whenever possible.

**Disposal of Unused Medications:**
- Unused controlled substances that cannot be returned to the person for whom they were prescribed are to be sent to Pharmacy Services at the Arkansas Department of Health and Human Services for destruction.
- A surrender form can be obtained from Pharmacy Services, 501-661-2325.
- Large quantities of non-controlled substances can also be sent to Pharmacy Services for destruction.

## Works Cited

American Nurses Association (2004). *Nursing: Scope and standards of practice.* Silver Spring, MD; nursesbooks.org.

American Nurses Association and National Association of School Nurses (2005). *School Nursing: Scope and standards of practice.* Silver Spring, MD; nursesbooks.org.

Arkansas Department of Education Resource Guide: Developing School Policies on Children with Special Health Care Needs (2007).

Arkansas Education Act (1999). A.C.A. § 6-18-1005

Arkansas Nurse Practice Act (2007). A.C.A. § 17-87-101 et al. www.arsbn.org.

Arkansas State Board of Nursing Rules (2007). Chapter 5 – Delegation. www.arsbn.org.

ASBN (1998). Position statement 98-6: Decision making model. www.arsbn.org.

Merriam-Webster On-Line Dictionary, www.m-w.com.

Wolfe, L.C. (2006). Roles of the school nurse. In J. Selekman, (Ed.), *School nursing: a comprehensive text* (pp. 121-124). Philadelphia: F.A. Davis Company

**For additional resources regarding school nursing and laws pertaining to school healthcare go to: www.arkansascsh.org**

—— **Complementary/Alternative Therapies**
(undated)

The competency of a nurse to perform complementary and alternative therapies begins with nursing education and ends with the safe nursing practice of those skills in such a way that ensures the safety, comfort and protection of clients. Nurses using complementary or alternative therapies in their practice should follow the ASBN "Position Statement 98-6 Decision Making Model." Particular attention should be paid to the definition of nursing in the ASBN "Nurse Practice Act," and statements in the ASBN "Position Statement 95-1 Scopes of Practice." Other professional practice acts may require additional certification and/or licensure to perform a particular therapy.

Most nurses have been exposed to systems, holistic and humanistic theories. These theories are the essence of nursing practice and may include complementary and alternative therapies. Nurses must practice within the scope of practice of their license. In basic nursing education, nurses learn to complement physician ordered treatments with techniques such as focused breathing and relaxation, massage, guided imagery, music, humor and distraction. The more complex complementary and alternative therapies are a part of advanced practice nursing. Advanced practice nurses may be qualified to recommend or prescribe vitamins, herbs, minerals or other over-the-counter products. The registered nurse practitioner and the registered nurse may follow protocols to recommend these products. These protocols shall be reviewed annually by the licensed physician and nurse and be provided to the Board upon request. The practice of applied kinesiology, herbal medicine, homeopathy, and ayurveda may require formal educational preparation and possibly even certification. State licensure laws regulate therapies such as chiropractic, massage, acupuncture and physical therapy.

Carefully following the ASBN "Position Statement 98-6 Decision Making Model" will ensure that nurses are practicing within their scope of practice. Nurses who choose to use complementary or alternative therapies in their practices may be requested to provide documentation that they have followed the "Position Statement 98-6 Decision Making Model" in making their decisions.

—— **Guidelines for Teaching Content Related to IV Therapy for Arkansas Licensed Practical Nurses and Licensed Practical Nursing Students**
(undated)

The profession of nursing is a dynamic discipline. Practice potentials change and develop in response to health care needs of society, technical advancements, and the expansion of scientific knowledge. The Arkansas State Board of Nursing developed Position Statement 98-6, Scope of Practice Decision Making Model, to enable nurses to determine if a specific task is

202

within their personal scope of practice. It is recommended that this model continue to be used.

**The Practice of Practical Nursing:**
*The delivery of health care services which are performed under the direction of the professional nurse, licensed physician, or licensed dentist, including observation, intervention, and evaluation, fall within the LPN/LPTN scope of practice.*

The performance for compensation of acts involving:
  • the care of the ill, injured, or infirm;
  • the delegation of certain nursing practices to other personnel
  • under the direction of a registered professional nurse, an advanced practice nurse, a licensed physician or a licensed dentist, which acts do not require the substantial specialized skill, judgment, and knowledge required in professional nursing. ACA § 17-87-102(5)

**The Practice of Psychiatric Technician Nursing**:
The performance for compensation of acts involving:
  • the care of the physically and mentally ill, retarded, injured, or infirm;
  • the delegation of certain nursing practices to other personnel
  • the carrying out of medical orders under the direction of a registered professional nurse, an advanced practice nurse, a licensed physician or a licensed dentist, where such activities do not require the substantial specialized skill, judgment, and knowledge required in professional nursing. **ACA § 17-87-102(6)**

Over time, it has become generally acceptable practice for the RN to delegate certain tasks related to intravenous therapy to LPNs and LPTNs who have completed training and have validated competencies. RNs are prohibited from delegating tasks that require the substantial specialized skill, judgment, and knowledge required in professional nursing to an LPN or LPTN.

**Minimum training for the LPN, LPTN, or LPN student who will be delegated IV therapy should include:**

Anatomy and physiology;

Fluid & Electrolyte Balance;

Equipment & procedures in intravenous therapy;

Complications, prevention, and nursing interventions;

Introducing a peripheral intravenous device on an adult client;

Set-up, replace and remove intravenous tubing for gravity flow and/or pump infusion;

Perform intravenous infusion calculations and adjust flow rates on intravenous fluids;

Monitoring the administration of blood and blood products;

Administration of medications through a peripheral intravenous catheter by intravenous piggyback or intravenous push provided the medication does not require the substantial specialized skill, judgment, and knowledge required in professional nursing.

References:
*National Council State Boards of Nursing 2003 LPN/VN Practice Analysis*
*National Council State Boards of Nursing 2001 Detailed Test Plan for the NCLEX-PN Examination*
*Arkansas Nurse Practice Act*
*Arkansas State Board of Nursing Position Statement 98-6 Decision Making Model*

## DELEGATION MODEL

The Arkansas State Board of Nursing realizes that certain tasks may be delegated to unlicensed assistive personnel (UAP) without a nurse assessing the client prior to delegating the task. These tasks are specifically listed in the Arkansas State Board of Nursing *Rules and Regulations,* Chapter 5, Section C. There are also certain nursing responsibilities, specifically listed in Chapter 5, Section E, which are prohibited from being delegated. This model was developed to assist the nurse in making decisions about whether a specific task may be delegated.

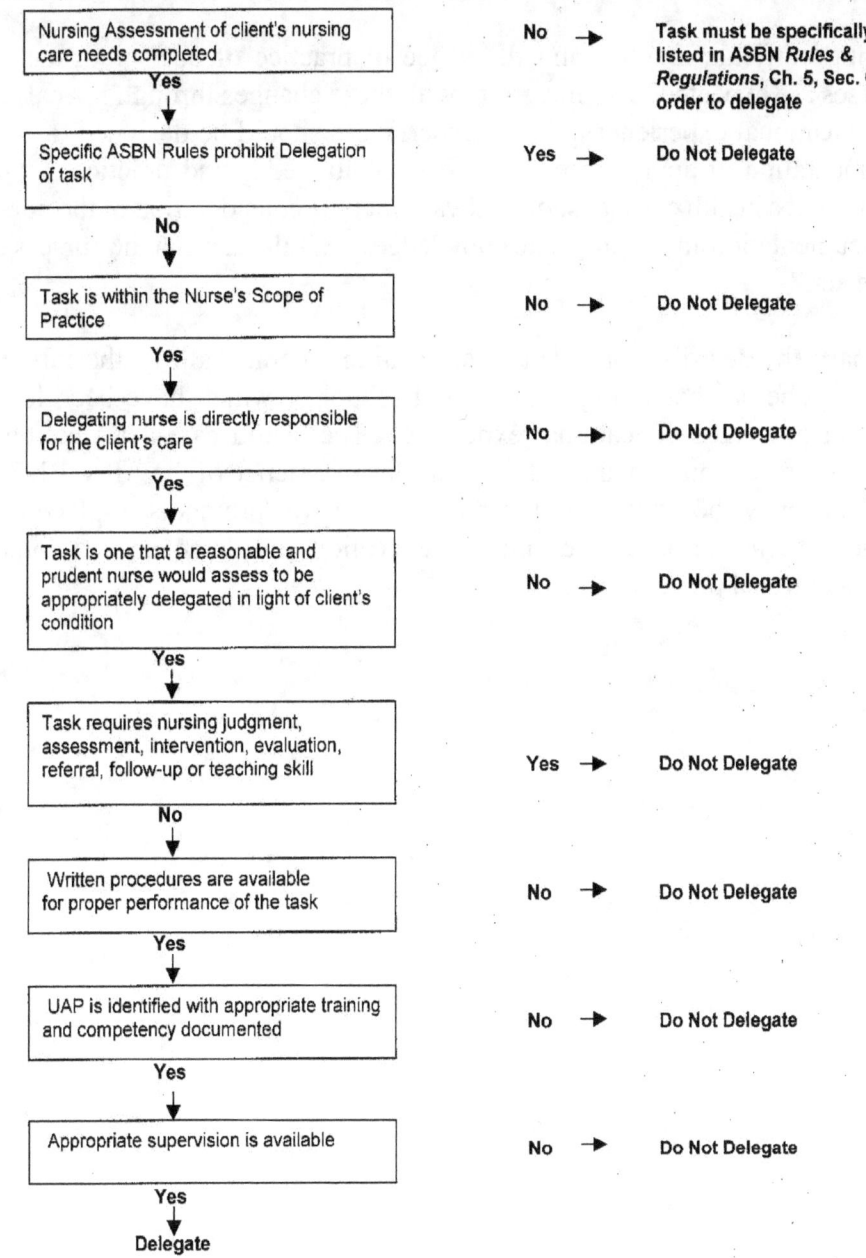

Nursing Assessment of client's nursing care needs completed — **No** → **Task must be specifically listed in ASBN *Rules & Regulations,* Ch. 5, Sec. C in order to delegate**

↓ **Yes**

Specific ASBN Rules prohibit Delegation of task — **Yes** → **Do Not Delegate**

↓ **No**

Task is within the Nurse's Scope of Practice — **No** → **Do Not Delegate**

↓ **Yes**

Delegating nurse is directly responsible for the client's care — **No** → **Do Not Delegate**

↓ **Yes**

Task is one that a reasonable and prudent nurse would assess to be appropriately delegated in light of client's condition — **No** → **Do Not Delegate**

↓ **Yes**

Task requires nursing judgment, assessment, intervention, evaluation, referral, follow-up or teaching skill — **Yes** → **Do Not Delegate**

↓ **No**

Written procedures are available for proper performance of the task — **No** → **Do Not Delegate**

↓ **Yes**

UAP is identified with appropriate training and competency documented — **No** → **Do Not Delegate**

↓ **Yes**

Appropriate supervision is available — **No** → **Do Not Delegate**

↓ **Yes**

**Delegate**

Adopted 9/12/96

## —— Sharp Wound Debridement
September 12, 1997

On September 11, 1997, the Board determined that conservative sharp wound debridement of non-viable tissue is within the Arkansas State Board of Nursing Scope of Practice Position Statement for registered nurses. The following excerpts from that position statement should clarify the Board's response to this question.

"Changing curricula may expand the scope of practice of new graduates over time. Practicing nurses are expected to keep current with these changes through formal, continuing or inservice educational experiences. These experiences should be designed to evaluate and provide documentation of appropriate extension of knowledge and practice… The nursing decision to carry out a health care act should always include consideration of the nurse's ability to prove by documentation and appropriate knowledge and skill base that the nurse is competent to perform the act."

In summary, the Board's scope of practice position statement allows the nurse to perform acts which he or she has been taught in nursing school or which have been learned since graduation in an organized educational experience. The health care act must be generally recognized by the profession as being within the scope of practice of the APN, RNP, RN, LPN or LPTN. Each agency should have policies and procedures/protocols in place for each act performed and documentation of each nurse's education and demonstrated competence to perform these additional procedures.

## 06-1 Pronouncement of Death
Approved September 13, 2006, Revised January 11, 2007

The Arkansas State Board of Nursing has determined that based on educational and skills preparation, it is within the scope of practice of the Advanced Practice Nurse and Registered Nurse to pronounce death. The Advanced Practice Nurse and Registered Nurse must adhere to other Arkansas statutes regarding pronouncement of death.


## 08-1 Expedited Partner Therapy
Adopted May 15, 2008

Expedited Partner Therapy (EPT) is "the practice of treating the sex partners of persons with sexually transmitted diseases (STD) without an intervening medical evaluation or professional prevention counseling" (Centers for Disease Control, 2006). The Arkansas State Board of Nursing has determined that it is NOT within the scope of practice of the advanced practice nurse (APN) with prescriptive authority to prescribe for a person with whom the APN has not established a proper in-person APN/patient relationship.

www.ingramcontent.com/pod-product-compliance
Lightning Source LLC
Chambersburg PA
CBHW081116170526
45165CB00008B/2457

* 9 7 8 1 4 5 3 8 5 3 9 8 6 *